The Trouble with Jesus

The Trouble with Jesus: Considerations Before You Walk Away is one of the most readable and insightful works about Jesus that I've ever read. In a breezy, hot-off-the-press, contemporary style, Constance Hastings brings the ancient stories of this remarkable teacher fully to life with clarity and breath-taking relevance. For those of us very familiar with the Jesus story, Hastings' unique ability to squeeze from the accounts more than we ever thought was there is enlightening as well as refreshing, even entertaining. Those who regard Jesus as Lord, the source and center of their faith, will be inspired. Those who see him as less or who've paid little attention to him at all may feel compelled to take another look at this Jesus who was always stirring up "good trouble." If I could have only one contemporary book about Jesus in my library, *The Trouble with Jesus* would be that book. It's that good.

—**Mort Crim,** ABC national correspondent,
author of *Anchored: A Journalist's Search for Truth*

The Trouble with Jesus: Considerations Before You Walk Away penetrates the heart from beginning to end. The author's written perspective leads readers to think of Jesus as an out-of-the-box figure, a teacher quite different from that which they might be used to, drawing readers into a deeper introspection of themselves and their relationship with him.

—**Joe Miller,** codger sinner saved by grace,
Cross Group Ministries, Denver, CO

The Trouble with Jesus: Considerations Before You Walk Away is a thought-provoking read. Many of the questions I have been asked over the years are found in this book, and I also discovered questions here that revealed new ideas and understandings of Jesus that challenged me to look deeper into my faith. As someone who has spent her adult life in ministry with young people and adults, I can't wait to share this book.

—**Gretchen Shea,** director of family discipleship and engagement,
North Raleigh United Methodist Church, Raleigh, NC

Jesus was a master at disappointing people's expectations, refusing to fit into their box of beliefs and behaviors. We want Jesus to fit into our boxes as well. Constance Hastings in *The Trouble with Jesus: Considerations Before You Walk Away* examines who Jesus really was—a countercultural Messiah who turned the world and our expectations of him upside down. This easy to read yet deeply thought-provoking work utilizes Hastings' compelling style of internal dialogue, giving voice to our skeptical thoughts to show us a Jesus we may not have known.

—**Rev. Dr. Rob Townsend,** pastor, Moore's Chapel, Elkton, MD

As I began reading *The Trouble with Jesus: Considerations Before You Walk Away*, I soon realized that I finally had in my hands the good news of the gospel as understood and written by an independent, perceptive, and talented author. Jesus, as the Son of God, is portrayed as a tragic hero potentially restoring life to all through his crucifixion and resurrection. In a captivating way, the author comments on what is going on in Jesus's story while urging the reader to join a troubling chorus of spectators. I am reminded how the angel of the church of Laodicea wished that its members were either cold or hot (Revelation 3:15). Rest assured, throughout this book the reader is held close to the fire while opening up new and needed perspectives on the many familiar passages on Jesus and the trouble surrounding him. *The Trouble with Jesus* will stimulate and enlighten modern readers who have puzzled over the Gospels and are seeking a new perspective.

—**Mark Johnson,** Ph.D. Experimental Statistics

Considerations
Before You
Walk Away

The
TROUBLE
With Jesus

Constance Hastings

NASHVILLE

NEW YORK • LONDON • MELBOURNE • VANCOUVER

The Trouble with Jesus

Considerations Before You Walk Away

Published in New York, New York, by Morgan James Publishing. Morgan James is a trademark of Morgan James, LLC. www.MorganJamesPublishing.com

Proudly distributed by Publishers Group West®

Morgan James BOGO™

A **FREE** ebook edition is available for you or a friend with the purchase of this print book.

[   ]

CLEARLY SIGN YOUR NAME ABOVE

Instructions to claim your free ebook edition:
1. Visit MorganJamesBOGO.com
2. Sign your name CLEARLY in the space above
3. Complete the form and submit a photo of this entire page
4. You or your friend can download the ebook to your preferred device

ISBN 9781636983387 paperback
ISBN 9781636983394 ebook
Library of Congress Control Number: 2023946940

Cover & Interior Design by:
Christopher Kirk
www.GFSstudio.com

Morgan James is a proud partner of Habitat for Humanity Peninsula and Greater Williamsburg. Partners in building since 2006.

Get involved today! Visit: www.morgan-james-publishing.com/giving-back

Contents

In the Beginning

Now, let's be clear about this. You can tell your story any way you see it. And I can jump in with my two-bit commentary when I want. But none of this "Believe it or you're going to burn" crap. I am only willing to listen because I agree Jesus's story might have some things I like about it. But it's my choice what I do with it. I've been given other belief systems about the universe, how we got here, and what it means to pass through this life. I guess, though, that I just think there's more. I'm willing to give Jesus the benefit of the doubt. And doubt is what I bring to this table.

A lot of questions don't get answered, and when I look around, when I look inside myself where not many get to see, those questions swell into doubts. I just don't know what to think about Jesus. You've got a different slant on him which merits a different take. Most try to make him somewhere between your best friend and/or a Marvel superhero who's going to make everything all good. But you talk like his middle name is Trouble. From what little I do know about him, trouble finished him off for good. So go ahead. Let's do this. Let's find this Trouble.

Jesus. If ever there was a contentious figure, he ranks at the top. This first-century Jew caused more trouble to both the Roman Empire and the disenfranchised Jews than any other leader or social/religious movement in history, either before or after his existence. Volatile tensions in the Middle East have brewed for many millennia. And Jesus defined some of it. Interestingly, while he had his followers, they were not among the movers and shakers of his day. His influence, though, permeated beliefs in a subversive appeal, undermining systemic processes in the culture. In the centuries afterward, controversy has continued around his life even as there are those who would downplay and dismiss his story. Starting even in beginning sections of the New Testament in the Bible, Jesus's purpose in upsetting and changing the status quo is announced.

However, too often his narrative as told in the Gospels are read as separate vignettes, just little portrayals of his life. This kind of reading, more often than not, leads to a cafeteria style of theology with an emphasis on "favorite Bible stories," a style that does not give the full message of Jesus's incarnation and purpose while on Earth. Diluted in this way, one is left with an impression of a meek and mild Jesus that is safe and sanitary, easily dismissed from the real significance of life. With that perspective, it is easy to fail to see how impactful, significant, and centered in deep meaning were his life and teaching.

On the other hand, when read in the broader expanse of cultural context, the narratives of Jesus's life prove to be dangerous. That's where the trouble begins. When this drama unfolds, his life is seen through a different, more clarifying lens. It is a perspective that stabs at the core of what is thought to be everything from common sense to established justice. Questions and doubts need articulation. Evaluation of possible results when his message is applied require scrutiny. When faced honestly, a decision must be made if one would become his follower and perpetrate the same kind of trouble that he started two thousand years ago.

Some parameters and background need to be understood. Although first century Palestine's culture was heavily dominated by Hebraic tradition, it was not immune from Roman and Greek influences brought by the occupations of soldiers, the resulting commerce, and the practice of pagan religions. While the oral traditions of the Jewish heritage were a time-honored practice, the framing of these tales, especially in later written form, adopted literary styles understood throughout the Roman Empire. Thus, the four books of the New Testament known as the Gospels, written in Greek, have elements of Greek drama recognized and understood throughout the reach of the empire. The structure gave a familiarity to the first readers of these manuscripts that aided their understanding of the message and themes of the Gospels.

For example, the fourth Gospel, the Gospel of John, begins with an introduction to the identity and character of Christ: "In the beginning the Word," which is later identified as Jesus. Unlike the Gospels according to Matthew and Luke, John's prologue does not deal with birth narratives. His Gospel almost makes those stories secondary. Instead, John's revelation opens with words which could be proclaimed by a Greek chorus, an outside voice giving background and insight into the action of the drama. As such, the Word speaks and is answered. This voice stands mostly apart from the action as witness to the narrative, sometimes adding to the tension of the scene. Ultimately, it frames who this Jesus is, and in doing so, it sets the stage for trouble.

This chorus voice has not died out, for the Gospels are no mere recitation of an ancient historical figure. They make claims both explicit and covert about God and the kind of understanding, relationship, and purpose known and revealed in Jesus Christ. An honest, engaged reading of the Gospels refuses then to be static, accepted simply at face value. It brings in alternative viewpoints, reasoning familiar to other worldviews. Emotional at times, it challenges the drama with its connection to the characters and the audience of listeners/readers from the setting of its time into later centuries. The contemporary chorus wrestles with accepting the Gospels' claims or rejecting them. For the message to be embraced, the presentation of choice must be maintained. Thus, while the Word was in the beginning, it speaks even now and desires to be answered.

> Are you saying I'm not the first to do this? What I have to say, how I say it, even the very fact that I am saying it are really part of Jesus's story? That would mean I can add my estimations to those who were there, those who have tried to figure this out, those who feel like me. Might as well dive in headfirst. Okay, I join my voice with them as they add to mine. God, bring on your trouble.

Further Provocations for Your Consideration

If you, too, relate to the chorus voice of Doubt, I invite you to add your thoughts, doubts, challenges, and emotional outbursts as you read. Use the margins to scribble comments, and circle words and phrases in the text. Ask honest questions. Go further and start a Jesus-trouble journal. Utilize the questions following each chapter. Add your voice to the chorus and enter into its drama.

1. What is your attitude toward doubt?

_____

_____

_____

2. What positive outcomes could there be when doubt is allowed at the discussion table?

_____

_____

3. What role does fear play in doubt?

_____

_____

_____

4. Questioning is doubt's sister. What is the difference between an honest inquiry and a manipulative ploy to deflect or avoid the issue at hand?

_____

_____

_____

5. How does openness to any idea that may change former perspectives affect wrestling with doubts and questions?

_____

_____

_____

6. For Jesus's message to be embraced, the presentation of choice must be maintained. Why must choice always be a foundation of this discussion?

_____

_____

_____

_____

The TROUBLE with Jesus Was . . .

1

His Prologue

Likely, the first sense of something wrong was heard in the pounding hoofbeats coming from the north. Fast and hard, the sound meant that the Romans were once again pressing the Jews for something more. Just a few years earlier, it had been a tax census, the Emperor Caesar Augustus draining them so the empire could have its roads and palaces. What more could their Roman overlords get out of them?

Helmets partially obscured their faces so that individual identities could not be determined in other times and places. Their purpose needed a mask, for with precision they reached out to steal the lives of the most vulnerable and innocent. Slit throats gurgled blood, silencing mouths that had been filled that morning with mother's milk. Knives and sabers speared those whose toddling steps could not run fast enough. Fathers' pleas and mothers' horrors only brought a more determined murderous fury. All baby boys born in the last two years or so in this place known as Bethlehem were butchered for the sake of protecting King Herod from his paranoiac fear of losing power. But the very one he wanted to eliminate was not among the slaughtered. The child's parents had left hurriedly and became refugees in a foreign place, escaping the trouble their son brought for now so he could live for another time and purpose.

This is what I mean. It's sickening that children would be slaughtered, but even more so, sickening that this baby, the one who's supposed to be the Son of God, escaped it and left innocent ones to die who had had nothing to do with him. Imagine the unsuspecting parents who saw their children die like that. What kind of God allows this? Don't we have enough to suffer with just to get through life? We have our own trouble. Jesus, don't bring us yours.

The Pattern of Trouble Is Set

The prologue in the Gospel of John states: "In the beginning the Word already existed. The Word was with God, and the Word was God" (John 1:1). This is no mere baby boy who rose to a small level of prominence as an itinerant rabbi. The chorus states in no uncertain terms: Jesus *is* God. As God, this Jesus existed "in the beginning," and, by implication, even before the beginning because he is a cocreator with God who formed the universe. His identity means trouble—trouble, that is, for those who would keep God at a distance, separate and safe from interfering with personal choices in life. It harkens back to the man and woman in the garden who, in taking the forbidden fruit, desired to be like God and thus, by extension, displace their Creator (Genesis 3).

John's prologue, therefore, sets the stage for conflict, a necessary element for drama and its trouble. The ancient chorus chants, "So the Word became human and made his home among us" (John 1:14). The entrance of God in human form threatens the human reach for control of one's life and destiny. Autonomy is challenged, for self-determination is confronted by a God who would interrupt human designs.

Even more threatening, called the Word, Jesus not only speaks for God even as he is God, but he also comes as light and love. To be apart from light is to be in darkness, and to be loved and experience that love, even in the condition of one's creation, one must become united with the lover

(vv. 4, 14). The trouble with Jesus is that he comes as a God whose love will change and consume one's soul to the point of being reborn, creating a new person who is foreign to that which natural and intellectual inclinations would lead. The prospect is not totally welcome, for although "he came into the very world he created, . . . the world didn't recognize him. He came to his own people, and even they rejected him" (vv. 10–11). Pushback erupts at the start. The chorus has set the stage for what was to come.

The Hero

Another necessary element of the drama is established. The hero must be one of high, noble birth. He is the Creator and the Source of everything there is (v. 3). His entrance brings him into the world saying, "The Word gave life to everything that was created, and his life brought light to everyone" (v. 4). Later, he would be called Savior, the one whose light would give abundant and eternal life. Full of grace and truth, unfailing love and faithfulness, he possesses virtues worthy of a hero.

Yet, there will be something in his character that will lead to his demise. In fact, his very virtue is what will establish the conflict. Darkness cannot exist in light, and truth, love, and grace threaten the darkness that abides by power and control. By subtle implication, the chorus foreshadows the trouble to come. The very attributes that make Jesus a hero, a cosmic being who becomes human and proclaims peace and love, will clash with the established order of the day. Trouble will be his destiny.

You know what? This sounds familiar. They say all great stories are really just one story repeated in different settings and times. It's what all good myths are made of. And all myths need a hero. Right from the beginning, it's clear Jesus can stand with the best of them, from good ol' Greek gods to Marvel superheroes. Yeah, let's settle in for this one and play with it. So what else have you got?

Adjusted Natural Order

Before Jesus makes his entrance into our world, the Gospel of Luke starts the narrative with an adjustment to known and expected physical processes. Zechariah, an old priest serving in the Jerusalem temple, is visited by an angel informing him that his elderly wife, Elizabeth, would deliver a son who will be like the prophet Elijah. This new prophet will prepare the people for the "coming of the Lord" (Luke 1:17). When Zechariah questions this possibility, he becomes mute, unable to talk again until the child is born. This birth to an old couple is called a miracle, one for which the childless Elizabeth rejoices. Yet miracles also represent adjusted order— when that which happens is outside the expected, predictable known order to life. Old women do not have children. Preceding the entrance of the hero, there is a reversal of reproductive functions.

This Jesus will reverse, change, and upset the world.

The impossible will happen.

It can only mean trouble.

Even more troubling is the hero's entrance. This time a virgin, a young teenage girl, receives an angelic message of another reversal. Without having sexual relations with a man, she will conceive by "the power of the Most High" (v. 35). Mary is "confused and disturbed" (v. 29) at the announcement. Beyond the questions of how this could happen are its consequences to her. According to Jewish law, if a woman was found not to be a virgin before marriage, she should be stoned to death (Deuteronomy 22:20–21). Mary's very life would be in jeopardy. For her to agree to the angel's proclamation—to say, "I am the Lord's servant. May everything you have said about me come true"—was to stand squarely in the face of trouble (Luke 1:38).

Thus, along with her cousin Elizabeth, Mary becomes a player in this story, the story which will shake the world to its foundations. Both women will eventually lose their sons to executions. By that which they are blessed, they will also know the deepest grief and trouble. Still, they believe the angel's messages to them. They are witnesses to "nothing will be impossible with God" (v. 37 NIV).

The Magnificat: Song of Praise . . . and Trouble

Shortly after the angel's announcement, Mary visits Elizabeth who greets her with words later prayed by Roman Catholics for centuries: "Blessed are you among women, and blessed is the fruit of your womb!" (v. 42 NASB). Elizabeth confirms that the source of Mary's blessing is because "you believed that the Lord would do what he said" (v. 45). Mary accepts what God will do through her. She then breaks out in a song of praise and thanksgiving, known as The Magnificat (vv. 46–55). The core of this song points to the trouble to come. This child she carries will be a blessing, but the blessing is for those who struggle. It is for the poor, the hungry, those who live in the margins, and it is a reversal of the status quo. For in this reversal, the powerful and rich will lose—and that will cause trouble.

Finally, Mary's blessing also spells trouble. She is the conduit through which this Christ, the Messiah, will enter the world. This divine act reverses the role of women. God could have come into the world in any way. Instead, the one who made the universe chose to enter through the womb of a woman and was born by one of the very processes that made a woman "unclean" in this early society. Jewish law had an aversion to female blood, and the process of childbirth rendered a woman not fit for contact with those in her company. After all the suppression experienced by women throughout history, the mother of the Son of God is blessed. God's action and Mary's yes to her Lord reverses the curse received by the woman in the garden, and the sanctity of life is affirmed yet again. Nevertheless, for those who benefit from the inequality of the genders, it means trouble.

Okay, this isn't all bad. Forget the virgin birth and old lady pregnancy adjusted-order miracles. Yet, in how the story is going, letting women off the hook for all that's wrong with the world, bringing them back as major players, and allowing them significance in history are where the world should be heading anyway. Yeah, let's sit with this for a while.

A Birth That Was All Wrong

For all the sentimentality that's pumped into the Christmas season, the birth of Jesus was mostly a story that came with more than its fair share of trouble. A close examination of Luke 2 details the tumultuous predicaments that came into play as "the Word became flesh" (John 1:14 NIV). All of Judea was under the control of the Roman Empire, and the order had gone out from Emperor Caesar Augustus that a census would be taken for the purposes of taxing the people. This tax would not benefit the taxed; instead, it would support the corrupt and immoral practices of the foreign powers in place. Everyone had to return to his ancestral center to be counted. Despite her impending delivery, Mary with her "husband" Joseph had to travel the rough road from Nazareth to Bethlehem, a distance of seventy miles. It was just one more way their people knew trouble and so were looking for a Messiah who would save them from this oppression.

Even with his faithfulness to Mary and care of her during pregnancy, Joseph had internal struggles about his relationship with her. Their custom of engagement was closer to being married except they would not have sexual relations. The promises and vows had been said. As any man would, Joseph initially had considerable reservations about Mary's pregnancy. Betrayal on her part would have been his first conclusion, and nobody would have blamed him. Yet, within him must have been immense compassion, for he was unwilling to break the engagement publicly (Matthew 1:19).

But again, an angel intervened, revealing how God was reversing order to save his people. "Do not be afraid to take Mary as your wife," the angel told him, "For the child within her was conceived by the Holy Spirit. And she will have a son, and you are to name him Jesus, for he will save his people from their sins" (vv. 20–21). Without saying a word, Joseph obeys.

Recall that Zechariah became mute after the angel brought news that he and Elizabeth were to have a child. Zechariah and Joseph, the two men most immediately impacted by these reversals of order, either have no recorded words of their own or are rendered speechless. Only the women have voice. Another reversal is achieved.

> Whoa! But that is good! Women get their say. The point is these gals were heard, at least in this part of Jesus's story. What an achievement, and the kid isn't even born yet. Beginning to see why you call him a hero.

If all was right in the world, the entity that would be later called "The Holy Family" should have had basic needs supported as their baby was birthed into life. Again, the overlays on the Christmas story today are often with pretty music, sleigh bells, and an overabundance of presents. But the real situation was stark. Mary and Joseph arrived in Bethlehem with no place to stay. Even with family residing in town, there were too many people and "no place for them in the inn." Mary delivered her baby in a stable, a place for animals, and laid him in a "manger," a feeding trough for a bed. She wrapped him in "swaddling clothes"—nothing more than strips of cloth (Luke 2:7 KJV). It was the "best" the world would accommodate for the Light of the world. This child knew poverty and trouble from the beginning.

The First to Receive the Gospel

Undoubtedly exhausted from long travel and childbirth, the family was not left alone. Shepherds ran into town to "see this thing" that had happened (v. 15 NIV). These men were not sweet little characters portrayed in children's Christmas pageants. No, they were a motley crew whose life situation was to do the dirty work for those of better social status. Today, they could be compared to those who work as chicken catchers for poultry growers, the ones who step into the filth of chicken houses and chase frantic birds before they are packed into crates and shipped to factories for slaughter and packaging for consumers. As outsiders, these shepherds knew both danger and cold in the fields as well as disdain from the society who benefited from their labor for food and ritual animal sacrifice for their sins. For them to show up right after the baby was born must have been like having a motorcycle gang run through the halls of a maternity ward. Their very presence would have been out of place and brought trouble.

Yet, they had a story that was from another place. Angels had come to them this time, and a glory, a radiance surrounded them. Light broke into darkness. Fear struck the shepherds, for they had no idea what this light could mean except for trouble. Yet one of the angels told them good news, the gospel message that the long-awaited Messiah and Savior had been born, and the baby was to be found in an unlikely place, a manger. The heavenly host, the armies of heaven, then released a cacophony of praise, saying, "Glory to God in the highest heaven, and peace on earth to those with whom God is pleased" (v. 14) The chorus broke in again.

The shepherds ran to Bethlehem to witness for themselves this child who would reverse the order of those who were dirty and poor. They told "everyone" what the angel had said about this child. Those who heard their story were "astonished" (vv. 17–18). Were they astonished at the shepherds' story or astonished that they would come up with such a tale? Could these men who were at the bottom of the social scale, these disenfranchised and hardened characters who herded dirty, dumb sheep, be the first to receive the gospel, the announcement of the Messiah? The passage does not say whether the shepherds were believed, just that people were astonished. No wonder! This was a reversal of how important, life-changing proclamations with religious and political impact happened. If true, it only meant trouble.

Nice intro here, baby Jesus boy. Sorry you didn't get the red carpet when you arrived, but Christmas songs would be lost without a manger. Oh yeah, we'll root for you and your shepherd boys. People of the night know things the rest of the world never see. Don't think, though, that your story is going to get much traction with a start like this. If you're going to make your entrance with people like these, then you'll get all the trouble you want.

Wise Men, But Not Like Us

The shepherds were not the only ones who knew this special child was born. Far away in another land and culture, astrologers/astronomers had seen a phenomenon that caused them to take a long journey. A new star had appeared, and they had interpreted it to mean a king was born in this country to which the star seemed to be leading them. Known as the wise men or magi in traditional Christmas stories based on Matthew 2, these men were foreigners and would have brought strange dress, language, customs, and a troubling presence in that they didn't look like everyone else, even with the relative diversity of the area. Their arrival in Jerusalem was with the mistaken assumption that the educated and powerful also had indications of the new king's birth. But this supposedly good news was received as trouble. No one, neither King Herod nor the senior priests in the temple, knew anything about it. The inquiry was taken as a threat to both.

The original readers of this story knew Herod and what likely was coming. It wouldn't be pretty. As a politician, he had built and improved many cities and municipal projects, but he also had to keep a thumb on the Jews who were not fully submissive to Rome, much less to him—not an easy task. Smart though, he manipulated the religious leaders to quell for the time being their desire to be once again a sovereign nation. However, Herod also was mentally unstable in his later years and notorious for being paranoid about challenges to his position and power, even to the point of killing his own family members. News of another king was a prospect that would require elimination.

Likewise, the high priests felt that they should have had some kind of indication if the Messiah, a king bringing deliverance, was born. Were they not the gatekeepers of the temple and the enforcers of Jewish law who kept the people faithful? They continually chastised the Jewish faithful for their lack of perfection in obedience, promoting the belief that it was required before the Messiah's entrance. Certainly, God would reveal this to them first. To be announced by foreigners, those outside the faith and their control, did not sit well with the priests.

Therefore, such intelligence, unconfirmed as it was, still was considered by both parties as a warning to their status and security. Not that Herod or the priests believed this story was real, but if others believed it, it could threaten their political and religious grip on power, wealth, and control of the people. Though usually at odds, Herod and the priests conspired in an unholy alliance about what to do with the report of this Messiah. Their pact foreshadowed what would happen thirty years or so later when political and religious leaders of the day would again conspire to remove Jesus. It laid the plot that was filled with trouble.

Just as the shepherds were directed to search for a baby lying in a manger, the wise men were told to search for this child in Bethlehem. The religious scholars of that day pointed to the prophecy in the ancient books of Micah and Samuel that this would be the place of the Messiah's birth. The wise men again observed the star and followed it to Bethlehem where it "stopped over the place where the child was" (Matthew 2:9). Time evidently had passed, for the passage now refers to a child instead of a baby. The family also was living in a house rather than a stable. With joy, these foreigners worshipped this child and opened their treasure chests of gifts. But again, modern-day Christmas pageants convey a different picture than that which would have been understood by first-century readers. Certainly, gifts of gold, frankincense, and myrrh are known to be lavishly expensive. Yet, the impact of their meaning meant trouble. Each gift carried its own significance for what this child would be. Gold was for a king, frankincense was for priestly worship, and myrrh meant his demise as it was used as an embalming spice. In brief, this kingly priest was going to die.

Symbolism. Good technique. Don't tell the story outright. Let seemingly simple elements foreshadow what is to come. Too bad you don't have some foreboding music to accompany the gift presentation. Yeah, your holiday songs just about hide the real story.

Herod had seemed interested in the foreigners' report, asking for details of the star's appearance. He requested the wise men return and brief him once they found this child so he also could worship him. Yet, Herod's intentions were not so honorable. Again, an angel intervened in dreams, warning the wise men not to report back to Herod and telling Joseph to take his family and immediately leave for Egypt because Herod intended to kill the child. With the provisions from the wise men, they left under the cover of night and stayed in Egypt until Herod died. The holy family and the Son of God became refugees on the run, compelled to flee for their lives. Trouble was at their door, ready to break in and bring death.

The juxtaposition of the shepherds and the wise men is just as troubling. Mary's song of praise had clearly declared that her child would be the Savior of the poor. The wise men, however, were very wealthy. Still, God had chosen them to have an integral part in the holy family's journey, for their call was to give safety and provision to this poor family out of their own "treasure chests" (v. 11). It indicates that the divine intention of the relationship of the rich to the poor is to provide vital needs and, in these places, give praise. Years later, Jesus would say "to whom much has been given, much will be required" (Luke 12:48 NRSVA). For those who would use their wealth just for their own benefit, it means trouble.

So the family escaped, but trouble was not avoided. When Herod realized what the wise men had done, he gave orders for all boys two years old and younger in and around Bethlehem to be killed. The prophet Jeremiah had said long ago, and the chorus in this narration reiterates, that there would be anguish, weeping, and mourning for dead children in this ancestral burial place of Rachel. The birth of the Prince of Peace ultimately led to the slaughter of the innocents. Horror and sacrifice, trouble in its sickest form, surrounded Jesus.

Years later, Joseph and Mary, again directed by an angel in a dream, returned with their child to Mary's hometown of Nazareth. Another messianic prophecy was fulfilled: "He will be called a Nazarene" (Matthew 2:23). But it also raised another question: "Can anything good come from Nazareth?" (John 1:46). Anything, that is, except trouble?

Further Provocations for Your Consideration

1. The comparison of Jesus to mythological heroes is not a major stretch of perspective. Does this concept help with your understanding of his story, particularly in these introductory accounts? If so, how? How does it detract from what you know of Jesus or have been told?

   _____

   _____

   _____

   _____

   _____

   _____

2. Whereas the shepherds were economically at the bottom of the social scale, the wise men, though wealthy, would also be considered outsiders for their ethnicity, customs, and strange religious understand-

ings. Yet they are integral to the story of the Christ child's birth. How do you interpret their significant presence in this narration?

_____

_____

_____

_____

_____

3. Mary's song and the angelic revelation to shepherds indicate that God's coming is for the poor and the suffering. The wise men's lavish gifts to the child gave provision for safety and escape from Herod. How would this emphasis find challenges in today's lifestyles and ambitions?

_____

_____

_____

_____

4. Trust in any form has an inherent tension in it. What does it take to tolerate that tension?

_____

_____

_____

_____

5. "The birth of the Prince of Peace ultimately led to the slaughter of the innocents." Though the story details violence and its resulting suffering from political power, it's no secret that pain is inflicted from many sources: disease, prejudice, greed, the need for control and power, you name it. People have cried out to God since the beginning of forever, "Why do you allow this to happen?" What are your thoughts around this fact and challenge of life?

_____

_____

_____

_____

_____

_____

6. How does suffering reconcile with the concept of a loving God? Or does it? If God is all-powerful, light, and love, why doesn't God stop it?

_____

_____

_____

_____

_____

_____

2

He Chose Losers

It had been another long night with nothing to show for it. He was a strong man, arms bulging with defined muscles, a complexion browner than his natural skin tone from a lifetime on the water. While he wasn't one of those chosen from Hebrew school to further his study, he'd had just enough religious education to make him a good Jew—one who kept the laws, participated in the festivals, and made sacrifices in the temple. He'd been trained but not given choice in life to be who he wanted. His father taught him how to fish, not because it was their pastime, but because that's how they made a living. To his breed, hard manual labor was his lot in life. Every penny he earned was stained with strain and sweat. Though others were fed by his toil, he could be easily replaced with another brute of humanity who would slave his life away on the waters with late nights and heavy nets. Life was no more than hard work, limited choices, and eventually death.

This morning was just another slap in the face. The cruel mercy of the sea had dealt him an empty hand that night, and now there was nothing to bring home to make life any easier for his family. Not a single fish. He and his partners knew their women would be disappointed. Others of a higher station would not be surprised. After all, these fishermen would never amount to anything. Empty nets meant an empty soul sooner or later.

On the shore, that new rabbi was getting ready to speak to the crowds. Great, now everyone for miles would know their failure. But Jesus motioned for them to come closer and asked for a boat. From a floating pulpit, his voice carried across the water with his message of good news for those gathered on the shore (Luke 5:1–3). But what kind of good news could there be for losers like him and his friends?

Every rabbi has a following, for how can one be a teacher without students? Teachers are supposed to pass on knowledge and wisdom, and the more successful the students become, the more successful the teacher is known to be. Thus, if one is to change the world through teaching, the best and the brightest students are sought after, invited to become part of the inner circle and learn from the master teacher. At least conventional wisdom would say so.

The trouble is, Jesus did not seek the conventional but seemingly called those who were not the most attractive or influential. On that day, Jesus reversed the lives of those who were on the bottom of the heap, only of worth if they made the rich and powerful look good.

"What?!" Simon exclaimed. *Obviously, this former carpenter doesn't know much about fishing,* he must have thought. "You want us to go out now and drop the nets again? Don't you know that fish feed at night, not in the middle of a hot morning?"

Even so, Simon calls him "Master," and out of respect for this popular preacher, he and his men push off in two boats again. Suddenly, the weight and pull on the ropes gets stronger. Simon holds tight, realizing the nets could tear. With the strength of years in these hard-working men, they pull and raise so many fish that their boats nearly sink from the weight.

Simon then realizes that Jesus is not one of those ordinary teachers who go around the country preaching and collecting money. He innately understands that this great catch is a reversal, or what the Gospel of John refers to as a "sign."

Simon had been noticed and blessed by one from God. Simon with his partners James and John, men not considered very intelligent, were at least smart enough to read this sign and were amazed. Falling to his knees, Simon begs, "Lord, please leave me—I'm such a sinful man" (v. 8). It had been beaten in him from both the synagogue and life circumstances that he wasn't anything of worth, meant to be noticed or considered special. Beyond what little he could bring home on a good catch, no one would have given him any kind of recognition. That's how the world was made; some got it all, the rest got leftovers.

Jesus leaned in. "Don't be afraid. From now on you'll be fishing for people" (v. 10). With those words, Simon and his partners, James and John, were granted a reversal greater than a boatload full of fish. They were chosen for a new kind of life with a leader who would reverse their status and make them into what they never could be—men who spoke words from God that changed lives. No longer would they be considered the losers, the bottom-feeders, the ones lower than underdogs. Immediately, they dropped their lines and followed Jesus. But what was life-changing good news for them meant trouble for those who always looked down upon them, those of status and power.

Jesus had to reverse not only the natural and physical world but also the likes of these men. They were not among those chosen by other Jewish rabbis. They were losers, and these were the ones called to follow and later pass on the wisdom of their teacher. Ultimately, Jesus chose twelve men of low social status. Most were either men of the trades or aligned with the Romans because they collected the taxes that supported the local regime and the emperor, dirty work likened to mobsters who line their own pockets with money not their own. One of the Twelve was of the extremist group called the Zealots. This Jewish group was committed to a militant overthrow of their pagan Roman overlords. The backgrounds of Jesus's first followers were so diverse that they would struggle to cooperate with each other. They would later prove to be of little use when the really big trouble came.

Oh, get real! These guys would never have been able to open doors of influence in a campaign to be light of the world. Think about it. Every corporation forming a board needs persons who can further its goal by their positions in the community. You need to build a platform, get people around you to promote you. These guys would shoot holes in that just by their association. Do you really need to start with this kind of trouble?

Desert Deception

This ministry of trouble began when Jesus was around thirty years old as a teacher in the synagogues in the region of Galilee. His cousin, John, had been proclaiming that one who would come after him would baptize, not as John had with water but with a baptism of the Holy Spirit.

One day Jesus had shown up to be baptized, and as John was bringing him up from the water, a dove landed upon Jesus as a voice said, "You are my beloved Son, in You I am well pleased" (3:22 NASB). Whether this revelation was only known to Jesus or evident to the crowd around him could be argued, but that's of no consequence. Jesus's baptism was most significant in that it signaled God was calling him. The human part of the "Word made flesh" was meeting his divine destiny.

The revelation sent Jesus into the desert wilderness—a retreat of fasting and prayer to figure out what this spiritual revelation would mean and the direction his ministry would take. He had to wrestle with his demons and face trouble to line up the real direction of his life.

Every hero has an antagonist who embodies trouble, and Jesus was no exception. By the time he met his greatest antagonist, it had been forty days since he had eaten. An obvious weakness, it's an easy play for his enemy. *Son of God? Change this stone into bread!* Satan challenges. But as one schooled in the ancient Psalms, Jesus retorts, *people need more than bread for their life* (4:3–4; cf. Deuteronomy 8:3).

Then the devil turns from food to glory. Showing Jesus the whole world in a vision, the devil makes his deal. *Just worship me, make me your God, and it's yours.* But it's an easy turn down; Jesus refuses with a basic commandment, "Worship the Lord your God and serve him only" (Luke 4:8 NIV; cf. Deuteronomy 6:13).

Finally, Satan makes it personal. He shows Jesus a life-ending that doesn't mean sacrifice and pain. *Jump off the highest point of the temple itself, and let the angels hold you from the fall. You'll have the people in the palm of your hand, and you won't have to end your life with a cross full of trouble.* Except Jesus knows what his enemy wants: beat Jesus now before he gets to the place where he'll beat me. With implied threat, Jesus finishes it, "Do not put the Lord your God to the test" (Luke 4:12 NIV; cf. Deuteronomy 6:16).

Ultimately, the devil retreated, at least "until the next opportunity came" (Luke 4:13). He backed away but did not leave totally. Even so, Jesus's victory was made in not succumbing to the wisdom of the world but choosing instead the will of God, the life of the poor in spirit, the meek and lowly, the pure in heart, peacemakers who are persecuted for righteousness' sake. The message for losers is that theirs is the kingdom of heaven (Matthew 5:3–10).

So you're saying that the panhandlers and other do-good troublemakers get in before those of us who've worked our butts off not to depend on social assistance? Can't help but think that your head really did get fried in the desert.

Hometown Rejection

Having established now a local reputation for good teaching, Jesus goes home to Nazareth. Teaching there would either bring his greatest support or his worst critics. The community knew him and his family. Though as a young boy he knew much affection, there still would be those with a long memory. Some would remember that Mary was pregnant before she should have been, and how the family, for some reason, had left the country and gone to Egypt of all places. Then there was that time when Jesus had been a precocious twelve-year-old, staying back in the temple in Jerusalem, sitting among the religious leaders and demonstrating a depth of religious thought beyond his young years. However, for all his young wisdom, he seemed to forget the basic "honor thy father and mother" part and caused Mary and Joseph much anguish when he could not be found for three days. He was likely known as having been a good kid, but maybe he thought a little too highly of himself. There were those who would have been pleased to see him take a fall. Those in the room standing silent and watching the narrative action begin to unfold would have been keenly observant of this fact.

From the Isaiah reading for that Sabbath day, Jesus reads: "The Spirit of the Sovereign Lord is upon me, for the Lord has anointed me to bring good news to the poor. He has sent me to comfort the brokenhearted and to proclaim that captives will be released and prisoners will be freed. He has sent me to tell those who mourn that the time of the Lord's favor has come" (Isaiah 61:1–2). He then sits down. The gathered faithful are impressed. They, and the chorus, watch intently. But his next statements go beyond their beliefs. Certainly, they hope with the rest of their people for a Messiah who would rid them of Roman oppression. Certainly, they have no problem with the poor and the blind finding aid and healing. And most certainly, they know their future depends on the Lord's favor. But what will this local guy whom they have known all his life have to say that could fulfill their own hopes?

"This Scripture you've just heard has been fulfilled this very day!" (Luke 4:21).

He claims to be the Messiah? Jesus knows they will pressure him for what the devil had asked—that he perform on demand the show of miracles that would back up his claim. Just as he would not succumb to the devil's temptation to grab power for himself, he refuses. No miracle would satisfy them. So Jesus tells them, "no prophet is accepted in his own hometown" (v. 24). Then he tells them that the good news is their bad news—the trouble that will follow him from here on out. He reminds them that their revered prophets, Elijah and Elisha, aided and healed those who were not of their faith and heritage. Their hope for deliverance was not for them alone but also would be for those whom they most hated, the rest of the world, the gentiles not descended from Abraham, Isaac, and Jacob.

Trouble explodes. Jesus's own neighbors in the fury of a mob grab him and intend to throw him off a cliff. Chaos erupts. Yet, the conflict must be resolved another way on another day. The crowd gets their miracle after all. Somehow, Jesus slips away. But no matter where he goes, the stage is set. He is meant for the world, a world that will fight for him and over him, a world that will dispute his ministry and claim as Son of God for centuries to come. Jesus's message of hope would be carried by those who had only known loss and hopelessness, the losers.

> Jesus, see it this way. You were lucky this time, but on another day you won't be. You're the one who will lose. So if the only ones you can get to follow you are losers, let's just say you are a hard one to follow.

Children and the Childlike

Even Jesus's disciples, more often than not, didn't get him. They could not understand the radical message or modes of operation of their rabbi. What else could you expect from the likes of these?

Simon, whom Jesus renamed Peter, the Rock upon which he would build his church and to whom he granted the keys to the kingdom of heaven, pretty much earned the Most Likely Not to Succeed award. Why did Jesus choose him as one of the leaders among the other disciples when on more than one occasion he was chief among the screwups? Sure, he was the one to proclaim Jesus as Messiah, one sent by God (Luke 9:20). But he also was the one who started to sink into the sea when he took his eyes off Jesus (Matthew 14:30). When Jesus appeared on the mountaintop with Moses and Elijah, Peter got the significance of the event all wrong and wanted to build shrines for each of the three prophets (17:2–13). At one point, Jesus even said to Peter, "Get behind me, Satan!" (16:23 NIV). Then, when the worst finally came, Peter with James and John slept while Jesus faced his coming agony in the garden (Mark 14:37), and with his sword, Peter cut off the ear of the high priest's servant, thereby earning a last rebuke from his teacher, Jesus: "Those who use the sword will die by the sword" (Matthew 26:52). Finally, Peter had sworn that he was ready to die for Jesus, but he not only deserted Jesus when the soldiers came; he became three times the coward by denying he had ever known Jesus (vv. 69–75). What a waste of effort for a follower who should have been let go at the outset. This Jesus asks for trouble.

> Yeah, send Peter back to fishing. This guy doesn't make the cut.

Now, to be fair, like the rest of the Jews, Jesus's disciples felt that the restoration of the nation could only be accomplished by a Messiah, a leader who would overturn the oppression that had gone on for too long. Even after their ancestors had returned from the exile and rebuilt the temple, the nation had always been under the thumb of another power in one way or another. They needed a son of David to bring justice and peace.

So while these twelve men followed him for three years, largely it was under the assumption that their rabbi would be that one, that long expected Messiah. Either in the lives they had now or in the eternal kingdom of God, they anticipated their reversal would be one of position, to sit on his right hand as a powerful deputy of the Almighty. Those closest to Jesus did not see the trouble they would know because of their allegiance to one who gave them wisdom beyond the world and who healed with either word or touch. It was an allegiance that could very well be considered misaligned.

Three times the Gospel writer Luke illustrated their misunderstanding. Being with Jesus had given them a different perspective of themselves, a perspective that elevated them above the low, working-class status they held when Jesus first called them. In a subtle way, they adopted a pride not unlike the religious leaders who very frequently criticized their rabbi. In doing so, their Jesus had another lesson to teach.

The disciples argue among themselves over who will be the greatest in the kingdom to come (Luke 9:46). They asked the wrong question, or maybe a question answered only to show an attitude that needed correction. In response, Jesus called a child to his side, saying, "Anyone who welcomes a little child like this on my behalf welcomes me . . . . Whoever is the least among you is the greatest" (v. 48).

Children in the first century were not always valued. In their early years they required considerable care that had little return, for the death rate among the young was high. Why have emotional investment in those who could very well die before they could work and be profitable? Children were the least among the lesser ones of status. They could not speak, work, or carry any influence to further the cause. Yet in their dependency on others for care, they carry a trust only children can exhibit. Jesus is heard in prayer thanking his Father for childlike faith, and when the disciples prohibit parents from bringing their young ones close for a blessing, he boldly states that only a child's kind of faith will get one into the kingdom of God (18:15–17). The least become the greatest. Another reversal that slams trouble into the center of social and cultural values.

> True, people love the underdog. Jesus, you're the champion of it. Yet, to come out on top you've got to have broader appeal. A one-plank platform is one that'll break sooner or later.

A Religious Setup

His choices did not go unnoticed. The Pharisees, a Jewish sect who exercised much influence and power over the religious practices of the people, took note that Jesus went so far as to eat with "tax collectors and other sinners" (Matthew 11:19), clearly insinuating that he was not better than they. The Pharisees had been watching Jesus, noting his growing following among the people and hearing of these healings the people attributed to even just his touch (Luke 4:40). For all the teaching he was doing, he did not seek the Pharisees' religious favor. Jesus explained sardonically, "I have come to call not those who think they are righteous, but those who know they are sinners and need to repent" (5:32). A thin but definite line was drawn in the sand. This rabbi was not going to be a help to the established religion of the day. It looks like trouble. Trouble, that is, from which Jesus did not hide.

When invited to the home of a Pharisee for a meal, he does the unthinkable. He does not wash, a blatant violation of one of many cleansing rituals required for those who follow the over six hundred laws the religious leaders instituted for the faithful. A belief had developed that if every Jew went for twenty-four hours without breaking one law, the Messiah would come. A high standard for sure, but one in which the religious leaders had turned to their personal benefit for power, status, and control. They were the gatekeepers and enforcers of the law and had added such legalistic requirements that the whole system became nearly impossible under which to live. Added to that was corruption that oppressed the faithful. Worst of all, it kept people in their place.

In an explosive reversal, Jesus unloads on these self-ordained gatekeepers of the law. He calls them greedy, filthy inside, likening them to murderers and accusing them of keeping others beside themselves from entering the kingdom of God. "What sorrow awaits you teachers of religious law and you Pharisees. Hypocrites! For you cross land and sea to make one convert, and then you turn that person into twice the child of hell as you yourselves are!" (23:15). Repeatedly calling them hypocrites, Jesus declares these experts will know terrible trouble in judgment before God.

The line drawn in the sand becomes an outright attack. The Pharisees know they can do nothing right now about this troublemaker, for they are hampered both by the crowds that follow him and Roman law which restricts their power. But their reaction is no less than furious, and a grilling interrogation begins as they seek to trap Jesus into incriminating statements. The priests send their proxies not only to discredit Jesus but to turn either Roman rule or the common crowd against him. They don't care who will do their dirty work for them. Furthermore, they employ both their own followers as well as the supporters of Herod to get the undermining work started. The setup is smart.

And they are shrewd. They know how to get Jesus out of their way: just show the people and the Roman overlords how subversive he is. First, you lower defenses, and the best way to do that is suck up. They address him as teacher/rabbi, say he teaches about God without worry about where the results land, how he's impartial and doesn't play favorites. They want Jesus to think that his integrity is his greatest strength. Oh yes, they are very skilled at this manipulation game. Get him talking and let him trip himself up.

Then they put it out there: "Is it right for us to pay taxes to Caesar or not?" (Luke 20:22). It was a question full of guile, crafted carefully. They figured either way they had him. Get him on record as saying people should pay their taxes and stand back while an angry mob finishes him off, maybe even get a good riot going in the temple courtyard. Specifically, this despised tax was a poll tax. The Romans used it to build the empire, not just famous roads leading to Rome but also imperial palaces and governmental structures that made them look good. The worst thing though was how it was collected along routes of commerce, so it effectively took from the people's pockets hard earned money right off the top. Everywhere you went, you were paying taxes. People hated this for how it subsidized their oppressors, and if Jesus in any way supported it, he'd lose his base among the populace.

Then again, if Jesus said don't pay the tax, while the crowd would love him, he would be dead meat. Then let the Roman guard move in and arrest him for treason and that would be the end of him.

A frozen crowd waited for his response.

Jesus, it looks like you're done for now. Trouble you wanted, and so trouble you'll get.

Jesus likely went just as cold. Without skipping a beat, Jesus zeroed in on his inquisitors' intentions, and again he called them out as the hypocrites they were, doing what they could to protect their own power and position, not honoring God. With all pretenses removed on both sides, he requested they show him the Roman coin used to pay the tax. Someone pulled out a denarius.

Not smart. Not smart at all. Among the ridiculous number of laws good Jews were to keep every day, a big one was that no Roman money was permitted inside the temple walls. The issue lay with the image of Caesar stamped on the coin with its inscription, "Tiberius Caesar, august son of the divine Augustus, Pontificus Maximus." In short, this very coin declared Caesar was a god and a high priest. It smacked right up against commandments one and two of the Big Ten. Jews were not to worship any other gods, and they were forbidden to make graven images (idols) of any kind of god. And yet these Jewish tricksters had a violation sitting in their very own pockets? Once again, Jesus turned the tables on these phony holies.

With the offensive coin in hand, the face of Caesar before them, and the temple walls towering above them, Jesus gives them an answer. "Give to Caesar what belongs to Caesar, and give to God what belongs to God" (v. 25). Jesus did not bow to Caesar and the Roman occupation. On the other hand, he did insinuate that since the Jews utilized the Roman monetary system, then they, in effect, supported it with their commerce. They bowed to the maxim, "If you want to play, you must pay." Even so, their allegiance was supposed to be most of all to God. They were well aware of the laws of tithing—giving back to God 10 percent of their income. But underneath, the tithing practice mostly added to the welfare (and wealth) of the priestly orders. Subtly, Jesus calls into question if God was the real recipient of the people's faithfulness.

Consequently, the Jews who came out to trap Jesus ended up smeared by this nobody rabbi and his following of losers. The posse sent to get him slinked off, caught in their own trap (Matthew 22:15–22).

> You have to give it to him. Jesus is supreme master at this sort of thing. Media today would love how his statements could be pulled for prime time, clipped for just the right ad and purpose. So he says, Caesar and God both get what's theirs, and you're good to go. Just what is needed in this world today: good old-fashioned compromise. Keep it clear and clean and get on with it. Got to hand it to him though, even losers can find a lot to like in this defense of his. We might win something for a change.

Gentile Persistence

Even among those at the bottom is the tendency to believe you only rise to the top by stepping on others. Two thousand plus years haven't erased that. The losers of the world—those who have been discounted, enslaved, trafficked, brought to the ground by oppressive power—know it. As it is, if ever there is a portrayal of Jesus they'd never want to read, it's this one. It's the kind in which you either look for excuses (like who could ever excuse the Son of God?), or with which you are made to wrestle until you come up with explanations, honest ones that you're forced to accept whether you want them or not. If nothing else, the story proves Jesus's refusal to meet expectations, to keep his story clean and clear of controversy.

Jesus was in a foreign place, away from his home territory of Galilee. In a real way, he was outside his neighborhood, in that part where "good" Jews don't go. Whomever he might meet in that place was surely not of his kind. That could be why he tried to go incognito, sort of, keeping his presence quiet. To Jews, Canaanites were the "other." However, the plan didn't work. When a Canaanite woman came to Jesus begging for help, she had first to face the facts about her religion, ethnicity, and gender, and that left her with nothing to recommend in and of herself to him. No husband is mentioned, thus, no male support. Add to that she had a "demon-possessed" daughter. Even for a loser, she was carrying a negative zero. All good Jews considered illnesses characterized by mental illness and neurological dysfunction as possibly brought on by a parent's sin, a spiritual issue carrying a judgment. Why should this good rabbi and prophet pay attention to this kind of loser?

He didn't. Her cries, fueled by her desperation, rose to a decibel level somewhere between croaking and screeching. Jesus ignored her. As any behavioralist knows, ignored behavior increases its frequency. The disciples can't stand it. They ask Jesus to get rid of her. This is where it starts.

Jesus tells her he was sent first to help the Israelites, not gentiles. Gentiles, all non-Jews, the *goyim*, were the enemy of those who considered themselves the chosen people of God. This woman was not a Jew, so she was unlike Jesus and those of his heritage. Jesus seems to have forgotten his declaration back in Nazareth about how the hope of God would be for *all* people. His words and actions display the attitude of one raised to be racist, to not associate or see value in those who do not look like, worship like, have recent heritage and history like his, like mine, like yours. His attitude toward her confirms it as he doesn't seem to hear her plea to save her daughter. If she had a son, would her value and her child's have been different to him? Basically, if the oppression and injustice others experience isn't happening to us or those we love, it generally gets dismissed.

All right, but be real. Why doesn't she just go away? Or why do people keep bringing up what happened years, decades, even centuries ago? Just get over it for goodness' sake!

She persists. Throwing herself before him, she begs for succor and help. She relinquishes all dignity, making it clear this is going to take more than a "I'm sorry, and I'll pray for you" kind of response. It's evident this is not going to be resolved easily. Jesus has to make it very clear to her.

He does. He also makes it clear what some people will do to segregate their kind from those kinds of people. He uses a racial slur to tell her what she is to him: "It isn't right to take food from the children and throw it to the dogs" (Matthew 15:26).

Yes, Jesus calls her a dog. This "love your neighbor" thing apparently had some limitations. Women in this period, women particularly without resources and protection, were often victims of rape. Add in that intermarriage sometimes happened between Jews and gentiles (please don't romanticize this; usually women didn't get to choose their husbands). Either way the result was mixed blood births, mongrels, mutts, the B's of the day. That's how he sees her.

> Good God! Jesus is racist! What's going on here? The devil got to him after all. He sold out and will only pander to the crowd he's garnered in Galilee. Yeah, we've seen this kind before. Looks like there's a traitor in the Trinity.

Take a breath. This Canaanite woman has been slammed and takes the punch where it lands. She knows what she's up against, and she knows today is not the day to claim her full rights. Like more mothers than could ever be counted, she has first to fight for justice for her child. She'll do what she has to do.

So she replies to Jesus: "That's true, Lord, but even dogs are allowed to eat the scraps that fall beneath their master's table" (v. 27). She meets him where he is in his own cultural context. Some dogs were allowed to hang around during the meals, small ones tolerated like pets. He'd seen it and knew what she was saying. She isn't asking to change the world and all that's wrong in it. She only asks something for herself—a crumb of compassion and healing considering all Jesus had done in healing those of his own kind, sometimes just by touching the hem of his robe (14:36). She gives him a perspective by which he can consider her.

It pays off. "Dear woman, your faith is great," he says commending her. "Your request is granted" (15:28). Without moving from his place, Jesus heals her daughter. Healing comes not by laying on hands or calling out the daughter's demon but by a mother's faith. Her belief that Jesus was the only hope she had for the life of her daughter fueled her persistence. There was no way she could have given up. Because of that persistence, Jesus saw her faith—a faith that demanded she be listened to in her plea for help, a faith that would sacrifice her own dignity and self-worth, a faith that would cross all human boundaries constructed to separate neighbors and enemies. She came believing he could help her and laid it at his feet.

> Wonderful. But there remains a question. Why couldn't Jesus just see her need and heal her daughter? Why did he put her through such turmoil to get what any person could see? Was he testing her, seeing if she'd back off, reject him and his power? But why be so mean and hard on her and not the Roman officer who came asking for healing for his servant? His kind would just as soon as put a knee on the neck of any loser in his way. Sure, he also had great faith, but Jesus didn't give him a hard time about it. Or was it because the Roman centurion was male and had power (8:5–13)?

This woman had no chance with Jesus if power and position were needed to move him. She was called a dog for goodness' sake. She couldn't fight him on that, not in her time and place. If anything, she acted like the bulldog he called her and stubbornly refused to let go of Jesus until he gave her what she wanted. Her tenaciousness makes you think that if you cry hard and loud enough, you can change God's mind. Implied is that human justice is pitted against divine justice, and God needs a shaking from time to time to get there.

Or did something else happen in Jesus in this incident? Was Jesus changed by this woman in his perspective that he was Messiah and Savior to all peoples of the world and not just these God-worshippers? This meant no longer mere lip service to set him apart from the usual power brokers of his world, a rant against all that's wrong with the world, those who would leverage the power in the faithful for their own purposes. Restoring this girl would take something out of him besides the power of healing. This action would demonstrate how radical his ministry is. What effect would it have on those who did follow him? Would they desert him?

Or rather, was there something here that was inherent in Jesus's ministry, something defined by his teaching, preaching, and healing? Each was vital in expressing how he brought a new realization of God's love for the world. He knew as much as any the struggles of the oppressed, the poor, the sick, and the powerless. Yet he also knew that the human desire for power and control over others could only be dismantled by his example. An insidious grasp to be better and look down on others infects everyone. If any needed to learn to live another way, his disciples, his closest followers, had to see it first from him. When he called her a dog after she'd been such a pest, you can just about see the disciples with arms folded across their chests snicker at how he'd given her what she deserved, that he had put her in her place. Jesus had done what they had wanted to do. He had modeled them at their worst, a place of privilege from which they could dismiss and deride others unlike them. These losers he had called didn't have it in them to extend a hand to those who were victims of that prejudice they had experienced as well. Yeah, it was bad.

Interestingly, however, while Jesus was one who could debate with the best of the religious leaders, it was a woman who showed him the fallacy in that position. He accepted it by her appeal to what was right for all persons. He knew it was based in what he could do, not only in a dramatic exorcism of a young girl, but in a greater exorcism of injustice in the world, a change and reversal beyond the deep and heartfelt needs of a mother and her little girl. By a woman's faith in him to be more than what the world would give to her, Jesus's example of love and grace heals and raises the reach of God's love (Mark 7:24–29).

Below Expectations?

Yes, Jesus was smart on his feet in debate, pushing his opponents to declare for him what needed to be said. In the end, everyone knows that accomplished leadership requires the right kind of alliances to succeed. For someone who would be hailed as Messiah, this king did not appear to know how to assemble the right kind of advisors. The trouble with Jesus began in the tension he created by not being a Messiah among the power brokers of the day, the people who could get things done. Rejected by those who should have supported him the most, he chose to fulfill his mother's Magnificat, siding with the poor, the sick, the outsiders, and he called failures who had no power or position to follow him.

Not a smart business plan on the surface, but even more so it's a deeper insult to those who feel elevated by title and position. Instead, Jesus blatantly attacked power structures and that made him an outsider. He called children, those who love best when loved most, unto himself. He loved the unlovable, and by extension, he demonstrated that all persons who would be loved by God inherently have that which makes them unlovable. To be loved by this Son of God, one must become counted among the childlike losers. Insulted and threatened by what Jesus was doing in the lives of those around him, antagonists, both of this world and beyond, saw him as trouble. The stage would soon be set to remove him.

Further Provocations for Your Consideration

1. "To be loved by this Son of God, one must become counted among the childlike losers." The trouble is that Jesus doesn't seek the conventional but seemingly calls those who would not be the most attractive or influential. Clearly, Jesus's movement began and grew

among the populace. Yet even when threats to his life grew, he did not become complicit or compromise with the elite. What does this say about his mission? How does it enhance or detract from his message today? Where would you be considered in his estimation?

_____

_____

_____

_____

2. "Even so, Jesus's victory was made in not succumbing to the wisdom of the world but choosing instead the will of God, the life of the poor in spirit, the meek and lowly, the pure in heart, peacemakers who are persecuted for righteousness' sake. The message for losers is that theirs is the kingdom of heaven" (Matthew 5:3–10). What does this statement mean for those who are relatively well off and have a good measure of position and status? Is it exclusive or expansive? In what way?

_____

_____

_____

_____

3. Poverty, hopelessness, and despair often lead to mindsets and identities that produce emotional and spiritual depression. How does Jesus's story and message speak to those who are "losers" by most estimations?

_____

_____

_____

_____

4. "Give to Caesar what belongs to Caesar, and give to God what belongs to God." On the surface, this looks like compromise, a good way to get along by going along in the world and still satisfy God. Can you separate what in the world "belongs" to God and what "belongs"—that is, fully owned by anyone else? How does such a concept challenge one's sense of possessions and wealth?

_____

_____

_____

_____

5. A frantic woman desperate for the healing of her child is rebuffed and called a racial slur by Jesus. Eventually he healed the woman's daughter, but what is your impression of Jesus in this situation? If he was acting out what the prejudiced behavior of the privileged looked like, did it lead to a positive impact? Is Jesus to be excused here, or is this unconventional scene of healing speaking about more than divine power to affect one person?

_____

_____

_____

_____

_____

_____

3

He Talked Too Much about Money

Walking into the temple during the Passover holidays, Jesus's stomach likely turned. Jerusalem was teeming with crowds that week, and the religious leaders had tapped into the profit that could be had from the people's need of animals for blood offerings. The faithful who had come to remember their deliverance from Egyptian soul-crushing and body-killing bondage also found themselves at the mercy of others who would squeeze whatever they could from them for profit. The devout pilgrims were setup, and the religious leaders had their cut in the deal along with payoffs to Roman officials. Extortion lined many pockets. In this place meant for worship of the God who had brought the Israelites out of Egyptian bondage, hawkers gouged the obedient poor who sought forgiveness from their merciful God. Only a Messiah could deliver the oppressed.

As Jesus held a whip, maybe he knew another whip would be slashed against his own back in three years' time. But for now, his anger erupted at how the faithful were being raked over in a desecration of the temple's holy purpose. In a nearly mad fury, he snapped the whip and threw out the greedy dealers. Sacrificial animals released from cages shrieked. Currency spilled and clanged on the temple court floor as money changers' tables tumbled over (John 2:13–16). Was there nothing this troublemaker would not do?

> Yeah, you're angry. But can't you see this is how the world works, how the wheels of power and influence are greased by profit and greed? You know, some of this could be yours if you'd let the shrewd operators help you.

If all Jesus did was to claim he was the Messiah, the story would have ended there. After all, his family background was questionable, his hometown of Nazareth was known for its losers, he insulted the powerful, and his closest relationships were not assets for success. Beyond healing miracles which he sometimes stingily performed due to others' lack of faith and belief in who he was (Matthew 13:57–58; Mark 6:5), he would have been regulated to the crowd of those who claim to know God but somehow just could not get it together in their own lives. This hero would have gone down in history as a pest but not much more.

If being a pest was all he was meant to be, then he certainly was good at it. Breaking rules of ritual cleansing was one thing, but challenging what sat at the heart of power and influence was another. All progressing civilizations sooner or later evolve into a society that garners possessions and/or creates a financial system to accumulate beyond basic human needs. Respectable greed drives business and commerce, and in some ways materialism highlights a society's true values and the lack thereof of genuine morality.

Wealth and Relationship

In first-century Palestine, people believed in the economic concept of limited good. The belief was that all goods, riches, and resources, as well as blessings, such as love, honor, health, or friendship, were restricted and fixed. In other words, none of this could be increased, including wealth, and the only way to obtain more for oneself was for someone else to lose what they had or give it to others. If you were rich in any of these ways, you could consider yourself blessed. Yet if you lacked anything, your perspective of a just society would be one that shared necessities with others. Coming from a poor family himself, it was no surprise which side Jesus promoted.

The trouble was that Jesus couched all of this as a spiritual principle of God's provision. He must have stressed financial issues so much that people even came to him to settle monetary disputes. One man wanted him to resolve a dispute with his brother over their family inheritance. Whereas Jesus didn't give him a decision, he did answer with a principle: "Beware! Guard against every kind of greed. Life is not measured by how much you own" (Luke 12:15). He followed with an example of a rich man whose vast financial success necessitated building bigger barns to hold all the crops his farms had produced. But the rich fool, as Jesus called him, planned to hoard all for himself and to "Eat, drink, and be merry!" (v. 19). Heaven must have shuddered when God said to him, "You fool! You will die this very night. Then who will get everything you worked for?" (v. 20). In short, building one's wealth but not having a rich and deep relationship with God will end badly.

> Oh, good grief. What the heck is wrong with having your stuff? If someone works hard and has success, why not have it all? You want people to go live in hill huts or something? After all, God made us behavioral creatures. We live for our rewards, and now you say this is all wrong? Troubled man, you certainly are.

It's not the accumulation of wealth that's the problem. Jesus further illustrated with a story of a rich man (maybe the same one, who knows?)

and a beggar named Lazarus. The rich man's life was summed up in one word—luxury. You know what that looks like. Sprawling mansions with fancy pools and garages (modern-day barns) with more square footage than some high school stadiums. His clothes closet outlay cost more than a small college tuition. An army of employees was necessary to manage his estate. Opulence was just a mere fact of life. But for all we know, he'd been smart and ambitious and now had a life where he could enjoy the fruit of his labor. All of this in itself was not the problem.

However, not far from the rich man's door lay Lazarus—a sad, poor beggar who longed for whatever garbage was thrown out after the rich guy's daily feasts. So sick was he that dogs would lick his open sores. Whether that was because Lazarus couldn't fight them off, or it was his only source of sympathetic touch doesn't really matter. Mercifully, Lazarus finally died, and angels carried him to rest in Abraham's bosom.

The rich dude also passed away. Financial status never changes the final outcome. But the afterlife for this guy wasn't a golden chariot through pearly gates. His soul landed in Hades, the place of the dead. Otherwise known as hell, it is the eternal antithesis of all the rich man had known during his lifetime. Accumulated earthly wealth could not buy him relief from the anguish of eternal regret. But beyond the distant chasm separating heaven and hell, he saw poor Lazarus with Abraham and at peace and restored from the agonies of his life. The rich man pleaded for some pity, begging Abraham for just a small thing, like the scraps Lazarus lived on for much of his life. "Send Lazarus over here to dip the tip of his finger in water and cool my tongue. I am in anguish in these flames" (16:24). He now knew and understood how much Lazarus had lacked in basic needs. The roles were reversed; the rich man was not asking for a good deal, just something to relieve his torment in a small measure.

Abraham's reply was not kind. He reminded the rich guy of how he had so neglected to care for Lazarus. But more so, giving the man relief would not be possible anyway. Fates are sealed, and one cannot change how one has lived and the ensuing consequences.

Finally, the rich man showed some compassion, at least for his own people. He wanted Lazarus to go to his five brothers and give fair warning of what their fate could also be. But Abraham reminded him that such warnings are in the ancient prophetic writings. Even the rich guy had known them but evidently didn't think that they applied to him.

The rich man then said that he thought his brothers and others like him needed more persuasion, like someone returning from the dead. If they could have only experienced such a shocking miracle, then they would have heeded the ancient writings, "repent of their sins and turn to God" (v. 30). The pull of control and wanting life on your own terms can be as strong as a titanium lock and hard to break. Such is the hold of wealth on the soul. Abraham's (and Jesus's) reply, though, had a double meaning for the trouble it spelled: "If they won't listen to Moses and the prophets, they won't be persuaded even if someone rises from the dead" (v. 31).

> Well, aren't you the downer of the day! So you want us to just give it all away to any old beggar that shows up at your door? Somehow, this thing isn't sitting too well. If you give it all away, what's the point of working and trying to better your life? If everyone thought someone else would take care of you, who would even try to take care of themselves? Mister Messiah, you're not altogether getting through with this one.

Don't worry. Jesus had plenty more to say on the topic. At the same time, he emphasized what is known as stewardship, taking care of whatever resources God has given, whether those resources are few or many. In Luke 19:11–27, he tells the story of three servants to whom their master had entrusted each an amount of money. The first two reported their investment had shown gains of considerable quantity, ten and five times respectively. To each of these servants, the master rewarded great responsibility as governors over several cities. But the third servant had hidden the master's money "to keep it safe." Consequently, that money saw no gain. For not having any return due to lack of even trying to invest it, the master orders the money be given to the servant who had the biggest return on his investments.

Jesus postulates some key points in his illustration. All that the servants had was not their own; it was the master's money they were handling. The inference here is that blessings are not for the one who is blessed but rather for the ultimate source of blessing, that is, God. When called into accountability for what has been done with those blessings, the expectation is one of increasing their value. Furthermore, although this story speaks in terms of financial investment, the underlying premise applies to all blessings of good, whether that be money, health, talents, what have you. In brief, all blessings are to be developed and grown for the benefit of the master. Not one good thing is one's own but belongs to God and carries with it responsibilities of stewardship. Finally, these blessings will be removed and given to those who are faithful to use and increase the master's blessings upon them. "To those who use well what they are given, even more will be given. But from those who do nothing, even what little they have will be taken away" (v. 26).

All right now, Mr. Messiah. It makes good financial sense to position one's wealth, great or small, such that blessings of any kind grow. We understand God doesn't want to see his good gifts wasted. But again, common sense would say take care of your own stuff first. Don't get yourself into a place where you're a burden on others. That's being a good steward of what you've been given. Then take care of what you've got left so you can help those who may need a little extra. Can't we just leave it at that?

Evidently not. "Can all your worries add a single moment to your life?" (12:25). This is where Jesus's message hits the extreme. He tells his disciples not to worry about even the basic things of life, such as food or clothing. If God provides for the lilies in the field or the birds of the air, would God not also provide for those who love him? "He will give you everything you need." Just "seek the Kingdom of God above all else" (v. 31).

Be good stewards of the blessings God bestows on you and make them grow. Now that's a perception that sits well with financial advisors. But Jesus doesn't stop here. He turns his counsel into trouble: "Seek first the kingdom of God and his righteousness, and all these things will be given to you as well" (Matthew 6:33 NRSVUE). Don't hoard those blessings; rather, use them if only for a little of what you need and certainly don't build an accumulation of wealth to just sit on.

Really? Then what, oh Jesus, is all this work for?

"Sell your possessions and give to those in need" is his answer (Luke 12:33).

For first century wheelers and dealers, this Jesus was moving beyond just trouble, and even today the message borders on the radical. Capitalists raise accusations of socialism and all the fears of economic crash associated with it. That line in the sand gets deeper and broader for those who will follow him.

Jesus doesn't make promises of security in the world. Rather, he declares the kingdom of God should take precedence—a kingdom that assures security for all God's creatures. In that way, one's treasure and dependence on God are activated by one's relationship with the Creator. He measures that relationship with, "Wherever your treasure is, there the desires of your heart will also be" (v. 34).

The trouble with Jesus was he would not tolerate anything getting in the way of complete devotion to God. It requires a reversal again, a reversal of what seems reasonable in living life. A rich religious leader learned this in his question of what is necessary for eternal life. This was a person well-schooled in the laws of the synagogue, and when Jesus reminded him of the five commandments surrounding relationship, this rich man could honestly respond that he had been faithful in keeping them since he was a child. He had never committed adultery, taken someone's life, stolen from another, or lied about another person. He had also honored his parents.

Nevertheless, it was his relationship with money that held him back. When Jesus said, "Sell all your possessions and give the money to the poor, and you will have treasure in heaven," the man was very sad, for his wealth was considerable (18:22). Presented with the decision to choose between his money and his place in eternity, he walked away. Despite all his training and position in religious circles, despite all his "goodness" and good works, the first two of the Ten Commandments were what posed the problem: "You must not have any other god but me. You must not make for yourself an idol of any kind" (Exodus 20:3–4). And if the rich man would not release his wealth for his relationship with God, would his relationships with others, even with his parents, also be compromised?

Contrasted with the rich ruler is Zacchaeus. Zacchaeus was a tax collector, but not just a mere tax collector. In Ponzi-scheme fashion, he was the overseer of the ones who did the dirty work, the tax collectors who pressured the people for the revenue that not only supported the Romans but also lined their own pockets. Zacchaeus, of course, got a share of the collectors' cut, and his wealth was considerable. In the system of limited good, he was a taker of people's hard work, and he was despised by everyone.

Zacchaeus was also a small man, too short to see above the crowd that gathered as Jesus was entering the town of Jericho. Though wealthy, apparently Zacchaeus couldn't even buy a good seat that day. People were not going to give up whatever they could hold back from this despicable collaborator with the Romans, even if all they could possess was their place in the crowd. Familiar with getting around whatever stood in his way, Zacchaeus beat them at their game. He climbed a tree to get the best vantage point to see the great teacher who some claimed was the Messiah. He may have thought he was safe as he sat on a limb, above the crowds that would have stepped on him given the chance. No one would see him there, and he could smugly tell himself that he had gotten the best seat in the house. In spite of that, he was not out of the line of sight of Jesus, this hero who was said by some to be both a man and God.

As God sees all, Jesus looked up and once again did the unthinkable. He called out to this hated sinner by name. "Zacchaeus! . . . Quick, come down! I must be a guest in your home today" (Luke 19:5). Jesus had exposed Zacchaeus to the crowd, but his purpose was different from what they expected. Jesus called this man and asked for his honor and hospitality. He made Zacchaeus worthy of his company, certainly not what the people or religious leaders would have done. Unlike the rich ruler, Zacchaeus did not turn away. In "great excitement and joy," he led Jesus to his home.

For all the accumulated wealth Zacchaeus had at his disposal, there was something lacking in him that his great barns of riches could not bring. This short man, isolated from love, had been selected by the Son of God for relationship. Jesus knew his name, where to find him, and the deepest need in his soul—a need to be loved even in his sin. In his excitement and joy, this little man was like a child, and Jesus stirred in him that childlike faith by which a soul enters the kingdom of heaven.

Jesus's call evoked in Zacchaeus a change, a reversal of all that he was and all that he thought was so important to who he was and what he thought he had to have. Unlike the rich ruler and without being asked to do so, Zacchaeus declared, "I will give half my wealth to the poor, Lord, and if I have cheated people on their taxes, I will give them back four times as much!" (v. 8). His promise was one that would restore in great measure what he had taken from others. But more significantly, it would be a source of God's provision for those in need, his true neighbors. With this unanticipated reversal and outpouring of blessing, Jesus declared, "Salvation has come to this home today. . . . For the Son of Man came to seek and to save those who are lost" (vv. 9–10).

Once again, one who had much also had much that was required of him. He was to be the source of provision and aid to those who had little (12:48). It took quite a sum from Zacchaeus. Even so, in the kingdom of God, this little man now was truly rich, with his treasure in heaven. Thus, not only was the plight of the poor rectified, but those who did not even realize their lostness had a radical reversal of purpose.

> Wait a minute, Messiah man. How come the rich ruler was told to sell all that he has, and Zacchaeus got away with only half? Why was this kind of unfair burden placed on the rich ruler?

Fair enough question for those who want everybody to get a fair shake. Still, remember, Jesus only asked this of one man, the ruler. He did not tell Zacchaeus to give up his job, nor would it have been possible for everyone who heard and believed Jesus to leave all and follow him. What Jesus was fighting here was the power of possessions and wealth to separate people from God and his kingdom. Jesus asked for people to have the freedom not to be possessed by their possessions but to live in whole-hearted service to God. Thus, Jesus did not have to suggest or haggle even with Zacchaeus about the size of his sacrifice. He accepted that Zacchaeus was willing to rearrange his relationships with his neighbors, especially the poor.

Finally, in acquiescence again to the concept of limited good, it must be pointed out that from a practical standpoint, Zacchaeus needed to reserve something so he could make good on his promise to pay back four times as much as he had taken from other people. The reality is that Zacchaeus very likely may not have had a considerable amount left in the end anyway. Even so, he voluntarily gave of all he had for God's glory to help others. It is a message that moves beyond the attitude "you can't take it with you." If one is to have treasure in heaven, investment in the kingdom of God by giving to one's neighbor, especially when poor, must begin now. For those who think life's fulfillment is to eat, drink and be merry, Jesus's message can be hard to swallow.

As Jesus watched the rich ruler walk away, he commented, "It is easier for a camel to go through the eye of a needle than for a rich person to enter the Kingdom of God!" (18:25). Jesus is not saying that the wealthy don't want to love God in grateful giving. He observes, however, that they can be so tied to their wealth and possessions that loving God is all the harder because they have such a material abundance to love already. "No one can serve two masters. For you will hate one and love the other; you will be devoted to one and despise the other. You cannot serve God and be enslaved to money" (16:13). The trouble was, Jesus left no wiggle room.

"Then who in the world can be saved?" (18:26). How is it humanly possible to care for oneself and those to whom we have responsibility in life and still sacrifice all that is achieved in toil and effort for those who do not have?

When one realizes, "What is impossible for mortals is possible for God" (18:27 NRSVUE). Jesus's message challenged the system of limited good at its core—this belief that if you gave, there wouldn't be anything left for you. The fear was if you give to others, you lose. Instead, Jesus reversed it to, "Give, and it will be given to you. A good measure, pressed down, shaken together, running over, will be put into your lap, for the measure you give will be the measure you get back" (6:38 NRSVUE). He urged people to buy into God's will and participate in this reversal where God's blessings are immeasurable and meant for all to share.

Jesus is adamant about this, so much so that he even studied people as they placed their offering in the temple collection boxes. On one day, many rich individuals put in large amounts. Given how all currency of the day was in coins, it probably clanged and brought notice to the giver. Yet the one who stood out for comment was a poor woman, a widow no less, who placed two coins worth in the box. It was no more than a couple of pennies, nothing to get a treasurer excited about. But Jesus noticed and used her as an example for the disciples, saying, "this poor widow has given more than all the others . . . . For they gave a tiny part of their surplus, but she, poor as she is, has given everything she had to live on" (Mark 12:43–44).

Most people choke hard on this story. The widow's sacrifice speaks to her devotion to God so much so that whatever security she had, it did not lie where most of the world would have it. Jesus's assessment shines a light on how this woman's poverty contrasts with the rich. What kind of world is it that allows persons to get to such places of destitution when there is more than enough for all if shared?

> A self-centered and grab-all-you-can-get kind of world it sounds like. Jesus, who are you going after here? Rich guys like Zacchaeus get into heaven by just shaking out their change. They've got it, so they should. But the average guy on the street has to carefully watch his accounts. Are you using this poor old lady to shake down the rest of us?

In Luke's account of the Beatitudes (Luke 6:20–23)—Jesus's sermon on the plain as contrasted to his sermon on the mount—Jesus declares God's blessing is for the poor and hungry because God's kingdom is for them, and they will be satisfied. But he warns that the rich will know great sorrow later for they have their happiness—their heaven on earth—now. Hunger and want will come to them (vv. 24–25). Jesus's mother had sung praise to God for how the hungry will be satisfied as the rich are sent away with empty hands (1:53). Such will be the reversals that await those who suffer and those who neglect their suffering.

Luke in his Gospel compacts the drama of the days before Jesus enters Jerusalem to meet his destiny with repeated challenges to how a fiscal system and its maintenance grips the soul. Another illustration juxtaposes two men of relative wealth. A Pharisee is in the temple praying—praying by himself no less. He positions himself away from the people because they aren't like him. They don't keep the fine points of the law like tithing. He's a good man, after all. He fasts twice a week, he doesn't cheat, and he doesn't commit adultery. He reminds God in his prayer how he doesn't sin. He even thanks God that he's not like everyone else. God doesn't have to worry about his faithfulness (18:10–12).

In a more remote part of the temple, another man prays who "dared not even lift his eyes to heaven." He is a tax collector, like Zacchaeus (vv. 10, 13). Suffice it to say, he was an easy target if you needed to point out a sinner.

Jesus contrasts the two characters, for while the first prayer celebrated himself, the second prayer was of such remorse that "he beat his chest in sorrow" (v. 13). He didn't make excuses about how he was raised or had a family to support or fell in with the wrong crowd. He only asked for mercy upon himself, a sinner, one who was separated from both God and others (v. 14). Yes, a sinner as accused by that very Pharisee nearby, but also a sinner that he recognized in himself. You can't fall lower than that.

While at the core of the story is an example of pridefulness, it also spotlights how wealth and position conceal and corrupt the soul. To keep all you have must have solid rationalization behind it. You know what that looks like, and Jesus heard it all even to his face. There is a cost to following Jesus, and it can be dear to the heart and soul. One person had declared to follow him no matter where he led. Jesus then said that he had no place to call his own, no home in which to lay his head (9:57–58). Implied was the question to this man, are you willing to forsake a permanent residence in order to follow me?

Jesus called another, but the man said he first had to bury his parents or, in other words, care for them until they passed away. Jesus placed his duty to preach to the living above all other priorities (vv. 59–60).

Another person just wanted to go say goodbye to his family. But Jesus told him, "Anyone who puts a hand to the plow and then looks back is not fit for the Kingdom of God" (v. 62).

Wealth is a significant example for many of what can seize and prevent a person from giving full devotion to God, yet any desire, even sometimes good and honorable ones, can impede, even chain a person from living a life wholly committed to God. Essentially, a desire for riches can contribute to spiritual blindness—a condition that keeps distance between God and one's business, much like the distance that the Pharisee put between himself and the penitent tax collector.

Jesus takes the side of the tax collector over against the self-satisfied and prideful Pharisee: "I tell you, this sinner, not the Pharisee, returned home justified before God. For those who exalt themselves will be humbled, and those who humble themselves will be exalted" (18:14). His messages always end like this in a spin of reversal. When you've done all you can for God, don't take credit or dare to touch the glory. Your goodness doesn't even come close to what God wants of you. Jesus wants that beating of the chest to be for what you haven't been, not for your own sake or pride but only because a broken heart is a heart that God can change. Now that is good.

Beyond these two characters, as always, others are significant in the telling of this story. Jesus speaks to "some who had great confidence in their own righteousness and scorned everyone else" (v. 9). It's not hard to guess who they were—those religious spies who often stood on the perimeter as Jesus taught. They were there to collect data and spin how this popular self-called rabbi was up to no good—or at least the goodness they thought was enough to please God. If good people were of no use to Jesus, then neither were they. This day only accomplished another mark of trouble between them.

> Even so, Jesus, why not leave it at that? Just show two extreme characters in their spiritual states and tell people to beware of being like either of them. Both sides would appreciate being able to take away something for themselves with their dignity intact. All this talk of money and pride, not seeing one's real motivation, and sacrifice of one's hard-earned labor for others. Jesus, why do you do this: shoot surgical knives into the soul and take away what makes the heart beat?

Not so. Rather, Jesus asks for a reorganization of priorities. His story of the shrewd manager is another take on what is important. At first reading, it may not seem to meet the mold of the high and holy. A rich man (who else, right?) finds out his manager has been stealing from him. The boss tells him to get his final account together because he's going to get canned. With that prospect, the manager does some quick thinking. Physical labor was not a recourse, nor did he relish begging, so he had to get creative. Now, here's the clever thing. He calls in his boss's debtors. One owed eight hundred gallons of olive oil. The manager reduced it to half that amount. Another owed a thousand bushels of wheat. That bill was reduced to eight hundred.

When the rich man hears about his manager's actions, he admires him (16:1–8). Jesus's commentary is likewise: "And it is true that the children of this world are shrewder in dealing with the world around them than are the children of the light" (v. 8).

> So Jesus thinks this arrangement, really cheating his boss even more, is a good idea? Seems like Jesus is getting a little shady here. And why would the rich boss think his employee was so clever and smart for ripping him off?

You need to come at this story from another perspective. Yes, the manager was a cheat and a thief. His business practices were not on the up and up. Today, the IRS would be all over this man's dealings. At any rate, he did get caught, and he was going to get fired because of it (vv. 1–2). It's the consequence for his choice.

But what the shrewd manager realized, albeit not how most people come to this understanding, was that he needed some friends and really fast. He needed them to be on his side, to take care of him, ones who'd be loyal to him because he had sided with them in their need. So he did that for which he'd soon be able to call in favors. He made friends. Now Jesus says he seems to have figured it out better than the people of the light do. It's another slam. Are you getting this now?

> Christ, but you are good at this. So the manager was the original make-friends-and-influence-people proponent. Wealth in the end is temporary, whether earned honestly or not. It's not going to last, even if you die with boats and boat-loads of it. But relationships, especially friendships, are better than piles of gold. Your people, the ones with whom you've shared stuff and shared life, the ones who will have your back because they know you've had theirs, will last.

Precisely. "Use your worldly resources to benefit others and make friends," Jesus added (v. 9). That point has already been made. But take note of how far it will go. "In this way, your generosity stores up a reward for you in heaven" (v. 9). Like the poor widow, God notices our sacrificial giving. And if relationships with people are vital, even more so is one's relationship with God. Money is a big, bad distraction from that. Again, "You cannot serve both God and money." God wants your focus, your devotion, your love above all else. For Jesus, money, wealth, possessions were illustrative of how that does or does not happen.

Time and time again, Jesus preached and taught about this topic. This disturbed more than the likes of tax collectors and dishonest business assistants. The "godly" Pharisees derided and dismissed the message for themselves, but Jesus didn't let them slide. He told them, "You like to appear righteous in public, but God knows your hearts. What this world honors is detestable in the sight of God" (v. 15).

> Well, dear Jesus, so much for making friends and influencing people on your part. You live for this kind of thing, don't you?

Yes, he does pile it on. Over and over, leading up to that fatal week before Passover, he taught these stories and lessons. The Pharisee and the tax collector, the rich ruler, Zacchaeus, the stewardship of blessings—no matter who he talked to or about, he wouldn't let go.

To Kill a King

Entering Jerusalem, a crowd spreads coats like a red carpet before him as Jesus rides on a young colt. The people shout, "Blessings on the King who comes in the name of the Lord!" (19:38). What happens is a real threat to the Roman order. A king not established by Caesar? A king recognized by the people who despise their Roman overlords? This is not good. It suggests the prospect of protest and rebellion, and political leaders and the religious leaders working in concert with them can't have an outburst of civil strife; not even a hint of it is acceptable. So the Pharisees tell Jesus to quiet the people (v. 39). It only raises their pitch even more. Jesus then tells the skittish Pharisees, "If they kept quiet, the stones along the road would burst into cheers!" (v. 40). Jesus refuses to quell the voices of his supporters. That shouts trouble.

Then the next day, Jesus adds more trouble into the mix. He once again enters the temple as he did three years earlier and drives out the merchants who line their pockets with money for sacrifices from those who have come for the Passover festival. Animals run loose, coinage is spilled, merchants' tables are turned over, and the system is disturbed and threatened—the system that oppresses the gentiles and the poor people who are there to seek God's forgiveness and worship him. Jesus once again upsets the way it's always been done. His accusations shine light on their scheme: "The Scriptures declare, 'My Temple will be a place of prayer,' but you have turned it into a den of thieves" (v. 46).

Yet another deeper, maybe even damning issue may have distressed Jesus more. The prophets had pleaded for it, but the Pharisees only exasperated it. As gatekeepers of the law, these religious leaders held their thumbs on the populace with ritualistic requirements that often were near impossible for the average person to meet. People learned from this that God cared more about the sacrifices they bought for their infringements than their relationship with their Creator. How people washed their hands was elevated above the love of God and neighbor. After three years of teaching and preaching of God's desire to be loved above all else, especially as reflected in the accumulation of wealth, and to extend that love to others in relationship, temple worship was still a farce. Nothing had changed, at least not in Israel's center of worship. That's what raised the rile in Jesus.

The religious leaders had had enough. They ramped up their plan to kill this controversial rabbi. Ironically, the priests would utilize greed to trap him. All it would take was thirty pieces of silver (Matthew 26:14–16). As far as they were concerned, Jesus had asked for trouble, and it wouldn't be long before he was going to get it (Luke 19:47–48).

Further Provocations for Your Consideration

1. We all know money is the grease that makes the world turn. Jesus challenges that assumption. How is the pursuit of wealth a detriment in his perspective?

_____

_____

_____

_____

_____

_____

_____

2. How are those who live in poverty also sucked into the world's view that money buys happiness? What does it do to them?

_____

_____

_____

_____

3. Social workers fight attitudes of learned helplessness. The poor, especially those oppressed by prejudice and racism, learn there is nothing they can do to change their plight, so they get caught up in systems of social welfare, taking help where they can get it, working the system to meet their needs. If God wants us to help the poor, how must giving and other kinds of help be designed to meet daily needs as well as change economic status?

_____

_____

_____

_____

4. "Sell all your possessions and give the money to the poor" is a radical statement. What is at the heart of this challenge?

_____

_____

_____

_____

5. Economics and capitalism drive much of our lives. If everyone followed Jesus's principles, what would be most challenged? What do you think would change as a result? How do you think those changes would be received and why?

_____

_____

_____

_____

_____

_____

_____

6. Do you think Jesus wants us to live in a communal system where everything is shared? Or are his principles on wealth and possession only meant as a litmus test for one's full love and devotion for God and neighbor? Explain your answer.

_____

_____

_____

_____

_____

_____

_____

4

He Valued Women

Born to a wealthy family in Magdala, she was gripped and afflicted with what was understood then as a possession by seven demons. Her mind had sunk into confusing delusion. Likely she terrorized all who knew her screams as she cut her body to release the pain. Her soul was lost to that which held her. Though there is no record of how he found her, Jesus delivered her from trouble with a healing that restored her mind and gave her divine purpose. In gratitude and devotion, Mary Magdalene was able to sustain his ministry with money and provision as he taught, preached, and healed with his disciples. She became one of several women who contributed out of their own measures of wealth and joined with him and the disciples as they traveled (Luke 8:1–3). Yet honorable in its intent, Jesus's service to and affirmation of women carried trouble as well.

Tensions surrounding Jesus had grown to the point that his life knew increasing danger. His birth narrative and relationships were not helpful to his success, and his affront to the religious leaders and the rich made life precarious. He needed support, and he found it in an unlikely place, given the cultural social limitations of the first century. Women—some of the ones he had ministered to—came alongside him and funded his work.

Yet it was because of his ministry to women that he also upset the status quo. The value he ascribed to women created a trajectory of freedom in rights to be ascribed to all persons. In doing so, he also set the bar high for moral standards.

For someone who rebelled against the fixed norms of religious life, in his sermon on the mount Jesus made a statement that seemed to adhere to what the priests plotting to kill him would want. They had drummed into the people that all of the over six hundred laws must be kept by all Jews for twenty-four hours if the Messiah was to come. Not one law in its smallest demand could be violated. So one's steps were measured on the Sabbath day, handwashing rituals were minutely followed, and the Ten Commandments prohibiting idolatry, stealing, killing, and adultery were to be strictly obeyed.

Right in the middle of his sermon, Jesus declared, "I did not come to abolish the law of Moses or the writings of the prophets. No, I came to accomplish their purpose. . . . So if you ignore the least commandment and teach others to do the same, you will be called the least in the Kingdom of Heaven. But anyone who obeys God's laws and teaches them will be called great in the Kingdom of Heaven" (Matthew 5:17, 19).

For once, he seems to be preaching the party line!

If only he had stopped there. "But I warn you—unless your righteousness is better than the righteousness of the teachers of religious law and the Pharisees, you will never enter the Kingdom of Heaven!" (v. 20). Another slap in the face to those who policed the people in the rituals of the law. He seemed to support the ancient laws given to the people in the books of the Torah, but there was something in his interpretation of the law that the best of the religious scholars could not fathom. His criticism would heap trouble on him just as he seemingly would support that which bolstered and held their religion. What could he possibly be saying?

Yes, the law still stands. Jesus was not going to change it. Instead, he expanded it. Doing so would not change the moral implications of what the law intended, but it challenged the religious leaders in the tenets of the law regarding their relationship with God. He would get them where it hurt, and so the trouble escalated.

The Unclean and the Dead

Now every Jew knew that the law of Leviticus was strict in delineating how a woman was made ceremonially unclean with each menstrual period. Not only that, but anyone touching her or that which she touched, even if one sat on a bed where she had been, would be infected by her uncleanliness. If a person touched her bed, one had to take a bath, wash clothes, be considered defiled, and isolated until evening. Washing and bathing were no easy tasks given that water often had to be carried, so this, in effect, separated her in quarantine for several days. Then she had to wait another seven days. Finally, to be considered ceremonially clean, she had to present herself to the priest with two offerings: one a sin offering and another a burnt offering. "So the priest shall make atonement on her behalf before the Lord because of her impure discharge" (Leviticus 15:30). Bad enough she was socially isolated for likely two weeks at a time, but there was also the implication that she was sinful for having a period. Under such circumstances, women were subjected to lives lonely and dependent on the rigors of the law. But the law, if violated, would impede the coming of the Messiah. There was no way then to protest but to endure.

Heavens to Betsy, you have to be kidding! This is abusive, horrific, religious tyranny. What God would want this? That she had no life of her own, her physiological make-up was a dirty sin, and let's not forget, with this cleansing system, everyone knew your business, even the priests. No one must have wanted a Messiah more than a woman.

Here again, Jesus gives favor to the unfavorable. Not only does he choose twelve men as disciples but around him were this following of women, such as Joanna who was married to Herod's business manager of all people, Susanna, and others who were able to subvert the system and contributed support for this rabbi and his chosen followers. Mary Magdalene, healed and whole, was among them. From the outside, Jesus looked to take on whoever would give him what he needed, and appearances were not important. For all his talk about not abolishing the law, he certainly seemed to think it was not that important when it came to women.

If all Jesus did was to allow women to be around and supportive, some people might have looked the other way. But trouble followed this man, and this man knew how to make trouble of his own.

One day a desperate father, Jairus, who also was a leader of the local synagogue, came to Jesus and begged him to provide a saving miracle for his dying twelve-year-old daughter. Possibly Jairus was so desperate because she was his only child. Having sons would have made her loss less significant. Still, with crowds surrounding him, Jesus agreed to go see his daughter.

But within that crowd was another female, one much older, and for the most part, knowing a living death. For twelve years this woman had suffered with a "hemorrhage," a menstrual period that would not end, a life sentence of being unclean. She had exhausted all of her resources, and still no doctors could find a cure for her affliction. Likely covered and heavily veiled, she sneaked up behind Jesus and touched just the fringe of his robe. Immediately, she was healed.

Jesus then asked a ridiculous question: "Who touched me?" With all the persons pressing around him, why ask? But Jesus insisted that more than touching occurred. "I felt healing power go out of me." Only one person in the crowd could answer his question.

The healed woman fell trembling to her knees. What was her fear? She had made virtually an entire crowd, and Jesus specifically, unclean. If the crowd was pressing against him, and she was so close as well, they also pressed upon her. Would her deliverance from this malady matter to them in comparison to what she had done to them? Her healing could have meant her death when Jesus called her out.

Instead, this Jesus who knew and did not seem to care about ritual cleanliness, called her "Daughter." He affirmed her efforts and desire to be made whole by saying, "your faith has made you well." Jesus made a connection between a synagogue leader's daughter and the value of her young life. For years she may have thought that she would have been better off dead than to live with a blood flow that drained her of everything, including the chance to have a life with any fullness. Jesus showed how much he cared for her. He called her daughter, and thereby raised up all women. All females, be they young girls or mature women, are touched in that place which distinguishes them as feminine. By faith women are raised up, healed of whatever wound life gives, and receive a transfer of power that is only of God. Then Jesus told her, "Go in peace" (Luke 8:41–48).

Before his words had barely left his lips, Jairus was told that his dear daughter had passed away. There was now no need for Jesus to be bothered coming to his home. Jesus, however, would not accept the news. He reassured Jairus, "Don't be afraid. Just have faith, and she will be healed" (v. 50). Later, among those who laughed at his claim that Jairus's little girl was not dead but asleep, he used the power of God to restore her to health as well (vv. 51–55).

Power transferred is power that heals. In one day, Jesus bestowed divine power on two females who could have been written off and forgotten by all around them. It was power for the powerless, and what more could get a person in trouble? Once again, a reversal of what had been before was accomplished, and it concerned more than issues of health or illness, life or death. Before long it would add up to bigger trouble.

The Crippled and Demonized

This teacher who had said he did not come to do away with the law would have to live within it, and if the religious leaders could find a way to show he was a violator, well then, all the better. So begins the drama of Luke 13:10–17, a drama with the stage directions left out.

The scene is set: Jesus is teaching in the synagogue. In first-century Palestine, whoever had that teaching spot had the center of attention. All eyes turned on him. He stood there with authority, not of his own but of someone invited to speak by the leader, the ruler of the synagogue. He had been given another chance to trip himself up.

But look where this drama goes. Another woman is there—a woman described as so bent over she could not fully straighten herself. She had been this way for eighteen years. But what is not said—yet fully understood by the first readers of Luke's Gospel because they lived in places like this—is that Jesus cannot see her sitting in the congregation. No, this seating was reserved only for men, with those of most prominent status and power sitting in the front. Where were the women? In the back, but not in the main part of the synagogue. They were outside the main seating area, behind a screen, probably a lattice. The women were not easily seen, nor could they see clearly or probably even hear the teacher well. The screen helped to maintain a caste system. Women, along with others who were sick or mentally challenged, were segregated from the rest of the assembly. It was as if those set apart were unclean.

That's when Jesus does the unforgivable. He calls to this crippled woman, recognizing her above the important men in the front. Mistake number one: in speaking to her, he connotes that she is a person of worth.

Mistake number two: in order to speak to her, either he had to move behind the screen to where she was, or she had to come into this place reserved only for the men. Once born into this system, you stayed in this system. There was no such thing as upward mobility. Jesus was challenging the system. Not a good idea.

Mistake number three: Jesus says, "Woman, you are set free from your infirmity," and then he lays his hands on her (v. 12). By touching her, he not only connected with her physical illness but also to the evil spirit that had robbed her of her health and her life. The sense of contamination was not just physical but spiritual as well. Jesus was really crossing some lines on this one.

So what happens next? She's healed and can stand up straight (v. 13).

> What's wrong with that? Her status is changed; she's no longer unclean. If that happens, maybe the whole system is going to be changed; maybe this synagogue is going to look a lot different soon.

And the onlookers were right because of what happened next. She praised God! A woman was speaking out loud and loudly in a religious assembly. One who had no rights over the better part of her life was speaking in this place reserved for men and only the most powerful among them.

What ensues next in this drama is the exchange between the ruler of the synagogue and Jesus. In a way it is reminiscent of the exchange Jesus had with the devil when he was tempted after fasting forty days in the desert. Both the ruler and the devil turned to the Scriptures to make their point, and Jesus's answer demonstrates how much they get wrong in their use of God's Word.

The ruler accuses Jesus of breaking Sabbath law, but to whom does he direct his charges? To the people, not to Jesus. Jesus was standing right there. Why not confront him face-to-face? It's triangulation—a tactic that those who cannot stand on their own use to sustain themselves when their support is weak. The ruler felt the full pressure of the conflict that was going on here. He was on the verge of losing and losing big. After all, if Jesus could heal, *and* they had just seen his power to do so . . . *and* if he could heal a woman, one who was not just on the bottom of the social system but was so low that she couldn't even look up physically, emotionally, or spiritually from the bottom . . . *and* if he could heal a woman on the Sabbath, a confrontation to the ruler's leadership, upsetting the very configuration of the synagogue . . . *then* this ruler was going to lose his power base and with it his prestige as a community leader. It's little wonder that he became indignant. His control and power were threatened.

Jesus was breaking Sabbath by breaking perceptions of what the social and religious structure of the world should be, wreaking and crumbling the caste system of the entire religious culture. His actions fractured and shattered a bondage which had kept this once crippled woman and those like her pressed and beaten down all their lives. These men, the synagogue rulers, benefited from this system at the expense of women and any others who had been suffering for years without any possibility even to ask for relief.

Jesus's response showed the people that the function of Torah and the law it contained was never intended to oppress people. Instead, as the central story of the book of Exodus declares, it was about setting people free for praise and service to God and neighbor (vv. 15–16). No wonder the people rejoiced at all the glorious things Jesus did. But after this incident, Jesus never taught again in a synagogue. He had "shamed his enemies" (v. 17). He was now done with them and their systems for good.

Temple Time

Well, Son of God, we like where you're going with this. This is something we can get behind, even though we're not all that ready to fully fall in step and follow, as you call it. Glad you got the heck out of there. Now, just set your tent in your own place, and we'll call it yours. See, then, what these Jews do when all these people they trample on go another way.

Sorry. That's not the plan. He will not walk away from those he loves. Abandonment is not in his rule book. Jesus won't be run off by these small-time tetrarchs. He's headed to Jerusalem. Stepping into the spotlight on an even bigger stage, that of the temple, he knows it's the site of the worst kind of trouble. He's ready for it.

But so are the religious teachers and Pharisees—the heavy hitters among Jewish leaders. They have their tussles with Jesus's teaching, saying he doesn't have the training, that is, the credentials they carry. But Jesus hits back: "My message is not my own; it comes from God who sent me. Anyone who wants to do the will of God will know whether my teaching is from God or is merely my own. . . . Moses gave you the law, but none of you obeys it! In fact, you are trying to kill me" (John 7:16–19). Nothing like saying it like it is. His comments put him in a bad place with the crowds. They need to act but not in a way that brings trouble on themselves.

So if Jesus heals a person on the Sabbath, and they can't catch him on that, then they need to go for the big one. Let him be his own judge, and let his judgment bring trouble on himself. Once again, a woman becomes a central figure.

This time the drama ensues when the Pharisees and teachers of religious law show up as Jesus was teaching to a crowd on the temple grounds. In their possession was a woman caught in the act of adultery. They dragged her to the front of the crowd and shoved her before Jesus (8:1–3).

Hey, wait! Where's her lover? You need a partner for this one.

Her accusers didn't think that was important. It's easier to condemn a woman.

With the stage set once again, they intend to bring Jesus down, again pandering to him by calling him "Teacher" (v. 4).

"The law of Moses says to stone her," they slyly say to the one who claimed he would not do away with the law. "What do you say?"

Would Jesus abide by the ancient laws this time? Would he support the law that protects the fabric of family and tribe? Or would he weasel out like he had done before on Sabbath laws? Either way, they could use his upholding the law or ignoring the law against him, and a woman's life was caught between the two.

Not answering any of them, Jesus stoops down and begins to trace his finger in the dirt. The story does not say what he drew or wrote, but they kept demanding he answer them. However, he knew their accusations were not altogether according to the law. Both Leviticus 20:10 and Deuteronomy 22:22 state that the man and the woman caught in adultery should be put to death. They only produced the woman. Still, Jesus doesn't protest the fact about her legal consequence.

Facing her prosecutors, Jesus finally speaks. He grants that they may stone her, but he gives them one stipulation: "Let the one who has never sinned throw the first stone!" He then lowers himself again to write in the dirt (John 8:7–8).

Tension builds. Which of those in the crowd could make a claim that sin had never sullied their lives? What judgment could be brought on them if they brought judgment on her? And what was he writing in the sand? Did they read in the dirt that which had dirtied them?

The oldest among them slips away and the rest follow, one by one. The stage is nearly empty except for the accused. Finally standing, Jesus asks her where everyone who had dragged her there has gone. "Didn't even one of them condemn you?" he asks (v. 10).

"No, Lord," she answers (v. 11).

Two small words speak once again of another massive reversal that Jesus accomplished. "No": the accusers have gone away along with accusations of guilt that she could not deny and for which she should have died, with or without her lover. Yet what the second word brings is larger: "Lord." There sitting in the dirt she acknowledges what she must leave there. As one who had little autonomy in this culture, she surrenders to the only man who views her with grace. Guilt revealed brought her to the only one who could save her—save her not by saying she hadn't violated a huge trust in relationship but by leveling how sin hides in many forms, not just in the adulterers' bed. She is saved from the consequences of her sin by a Savior who will now not just save her life but for whom he will save the rest of her life. Jesus is Lord, the Messiah, the God of supreme authority in the fullness of her life and for whom she must live.

He then affirms her answer. He will not condemn her either (v. 11).

Even so, while forgiven sin is huge, there is an expectation required by her Savior and Lord. "Go and sin no more," he tells her (v. 11). Do not return to your lover. Do not seek life as before. Change what has happened to you by changing yourself, reversing what you thought you had to have and needed. "Go," he said and continue in life. But "sin no more." Do not let yourself ever be separated from God and from others by your choices—choices that are moral choices because they concern holy and human relationships.

Thus, there in the temple where the law had been kept, stone tablets which had been written on with the finger of God, another finger traced out in the dust what the law was meant to be. It was meant to show life in full relationship with the Spirit of God and the spirit of family and friends. It gave not condemnation but firm boundaries set by God and not by human desire.

So it is: the trouble with Jesus was he valued women, and while he upset the traditional roles of gender, through women he upheld the moral implication of the law.

Friends, Supporters, and Family

Jesus not only preached an expansion of freedom for women, but he also affirmed it in his own relationships. He was friends with a family of siblings, Mary, Martha, and Lazarus. In their home in Bethany outside Jerusalem, he stayed at least once. Martha assumed the traditional female role of preparing a meal for their guest, and she was greatly perturbed that her sister did not help but sat listening to Jesus at his feet while he taught. When Martha complained to Jesus, he said that she was "upset over all these details!" (Luke 10:41). Details of work and the role of who is supposed to cook and serve contrast with details of how best to honor their guest by listening and absorbing his wisdom. "There is only one thing worth being concerned about. Mary has discovered it, and it will not be taken away from her" (v. 42). Jesus extends to Mary the spiritual and intellectual freedom to choose to learn from her teacher and not be regulated to that of a servant.

> Wait a minute, weren't women supposed to be kept in the back and out of sight most of the time? How did Jesus get away by having them around, supporting his ministry, seeing them as worthy to learn from him for their own spiritual edification? We'd bet people were whispering a lot about this one.

Plenty was said, and his affirmations of women added to the trouble. Each of the Gospels records women who brought their devotion to Jesus in costly fashion. In each Gospel scene, they served their Lord by anointing him with highly expensive perfume, sometimes recorded as being worth almost a year's salary or even up to tens of thousands of dollars. Yet while each account takes place during a meal, the homes differ.

Sometimes the event occurs in the residence of Simon, who is described conversely as either a leper or a Pharisee. Another time it occurs in the home of Martha, Mary, and Lazarus. Timing of the events also vary, sometimes reported to have taken place early in Jesus's ministry, then just before his triumphal entry into Jerusalem (now known as Palm Sunday), again right after Palm Sunday, and later in the week closer to his crucifixion. The woman in the story is unnamed in three accounts. In one of those she is described as a "sinner," while the fourth reports the woman as the devoted Mary, sister of Martha and Lazarus. Twice the woman anoints Jesus's head, and twice she anoints his feet. Finally, the response of those also at the table differs in their protest of how the money to buy the perfume could have been given to the poor. It is said to come from just those around the table, other times it's from Jesus's own disciples, and finally the objection comes specifically from the disciple Judas, who it is said really wants the money for himself. That's enough to make you question, what's the real story here? Who was this woman (or women), and when and where did all of this happen?

Some would say it only happened once, but the details in each recording are so distinct, it could be just as likely that it happened more often, at least four times (Matthew 26:1–13; Mark 14:3–9; Luke 7:36–49; John 12:1–8). Possibly, what's recorded is not a single story. Maybe it's an occurrence that happened more than once, each time seen and recorded with differing details because it wasn't always the same but every time significant to understanding Jesus as Son of God and sacrificial Savoir. Women of that day and time recognized their hero-Messiah, knowing by his affirmation of their lives that they could be delivered from oppression. To limit this to just one account is to limit the impact Jesus brought to women and the devotion he inspired.

These female followers also understood the trouble that his attention to them would cost him. These seemingly different women knew the love and power of Jesus, and in their examples of anointing with perfume, they foreshadowed what it would eventually cost Jesus for them to be forgiven. The custom of the day was to prepare bodies for burial by using oils, spices, and perfumes. Each of these women knew what was coming, anointing his body for burial, preparing him for what was to come. For this, while they still could, in their adoration they stayed at his feet and extravagantly demonstrated an understanding his ministry brought to them and those oppressed like them.

Yet inherent in their actions was also a cost. "She broke open the jar and poured the perfume over his head" (Mark 14:3). Here is where all the stories are consistent: for these women to anoint Jesus, that which held what was so precious and costly had first to be broken. Often this is thought of as breaking a seal or removing a cork-like stopper. But interestingly, the Greek word used here actually can mean "to break into pieces." It wasn't just an easy twist of the cap, but something that had to be shattered in order to access the ointment. Jesus used the same word in Luke 4:18 (KJV), "The Spirit of the Lord is upon me, because he hath anointed me to preach the gospel to the poor; he hath sent me to heal the brokenhearted." "Brokenhearted"—a heart that is in pieces, like little shivers of glass. More than once as they anointed Jesus, these women also did so with their tears. Something in them was shattered, broken into pieces, something you would think you would protect and hold dear, all this first before they could anoint, worship, and adore their Lord.

What these women exemplified in worshipful adoration meant trouble for the men and any who would criticize the expense of perfumes. The extravagance of their action was not just for the major reversals of status Jesus advocated but also for a change of heart before God.

> Really? Like these women had some inside knowledge the guys couldn't see. Stretch this if you will, but their actions could also just mean they wanted to honor Jesus and leave it at that. What gives you the right to make this more than what the passages say?

Fair enough. It's smart to guard against making Jesus and his life according to some agenda not intended. Since we live in a radically different culture and our worldviews are not of the first century, our lens has to be cleared and polished to see clearly and not color Jesus's story with our sensibilities of what we want it to say.

But here's what the accounts do say. Jesus himself affirmed in three of them that the women did it to prepare for his burial. Yeah, you're right. He's still alive, and they are like embalming him already?

Ugh. Sounds like a bad horror movie.

Perhaps more is also going on. Let's start with the fourth woman, the "sinner" (Luke 7:37 KJV). There's no mention of dying in this rendition. Jesus's offense in accepting her anointing is how he forgives her sins. Her costly administration of perfume was a reflection of what it would one day cost him in granting mercy and grace for her. Thus, when he accepts the anointing from the others, he accepts that they know the cost for him to grant that forgiveness, his very life.

Even so, though Jesus brought affirmations in the lives of women, life for them would not change for centuries. That movement would be a struggle for a later time, even as Jesus's relationships with women demonstrated their worth and value before God. By his teachings he gave them a form of protection in the major social structure in which they existed, and in this way he expanded the law above personal desire and need.

For most women in the first century, there were three life paths: slavery, prostitution, or marriage, all without any form of autonomy in their lives. In one way or another, a woman was the property of someone else (Deuteronomy 24:1). Thus, the lines between the three options were often blurred. A man could divorce a woman with no real cause, and the relationship within a marriage was not based on equality, a mutual honoring of each other.

Yet here again, Jesus heads for trouble. His sermon on the mount demonstrates that the law not only entails actions but the premeditations that precede behavior. Matthew 5–7 doesn't make full obedience to both the letter and the purpose of the law easy.

Do you hate someone? You could be judged for murder.

Do you entertain lust for another? You're just as guilty of adultery as if you had carried out the act.

Do you judge others? Expect judgment in the same measure you give it.

While Jesus does not do away with the law, he definitely expands it but not toward legalism. Instead, he focuses on the attitude one holds toward others: turn the other cheek, pray for your enemies, and treat others as you would have them treat you. "When Jesus had finished saying these things, the crowds were amazed at this teaching, for he taught with real authority—quite unlike their teachers of religious law." And large crowds followed him down the mountainside (7:28–8:1). The people followed him because of his power of presence in revealing the real meaning of the law, not due to any emphasis placed on the legal tenets of judgment that control and hold people powerless.

That could mean trouble in several ways, but it was his teaching on marriage that spelled the deepest reversal. He said a man could not divorce his wife unless there is an issue of her unfaithfulness. If so, he had, in effect, caused her to commit adultery. Putting a wife aside with no thought to the vows of lifelong marriage was unacceptable. That gave women a measure of protection, but Jesus goes even further. He tells the Pharisees that marriage welds two into one and that which God has joined together should not be separated. The relationship formed is not of individuals but a union which God has created, a union thus of three, not two. He echoes the ancient words of Malachi 2:15–17. "Didn't the Lord make you one with your wife? In body and spirit you are his. . . . So guard your heart; remain loyal to the wife of your youth. 'For I hate divorce!' says the Lord, the God of Israel. 'To divorce your wife is to overwhelm her with cruelty,' says the Lord of Heaven's Armies. 'So guard your heart; do not be unfaithful to your wife.'" Read and hear that this is not as a statement of anger and judgment but as from a hurting God who pleads for the marital relationship not to be broken and shattered. Jesus likewise makes it clear that God holds relationships primary. "Love your God" and "love your neighbor as yourself" were, Jesus said, the two greatest commandments (Matthew 22:37, 39). If love defines relationships with God and others, then the marriage relationship is the highest humans can have with one another. Thus "a man leaves his father and mother and is joined to his wife, and the two are united into one" (19:5).

Jesus affirms what the Torah had taught and implied in Genesis 2:24–25. Marriage is a holy relationship and designed to be an inviolable union, one formed by God. Thus, this union was not to be dissolved for any reason except for that sin which breaks a marriage relationship in the worst way, adultery—a violation in that day that was understood as any kind of sexual immorality. This teaching had been undermined by the religious leaders who had made divorce a command rather than a concession and had extended the justification for divorce to as trivial a matter as the wife burning the husband's food.

Jesus throws the day's accepted social structure on its end. As in all relationships, but most of all within marriage, love is central in affirming and caring for that person with whom one is joined. To love that person, then, is to fulfill the great commandment in loving oneself and loving God. Thus, the abusive practices of women being treated like property that could be disposed of easily are struck down. Instead, women are affirmed in their relationship with their husband and affirmed in their relationship with God. They can praise God in thankfulness, sit and learn at the rabbi's feet, and worship generously. The lattice which separates them in worship and forbids their voice in the assembly is struck down; their physical makeup which provides for procreation is not a point of uncleanliness that should isolate relationships; and God's law of purity and faithfulness is required, making marriage a holy union. The Son of God recognizes daughters for their faith and extravagant love, upsets the cultural norms of society and the religious status quo, and establishes high standards of relationship. For this first-century deliverance, he will know trouble.

Even so, as love and acceptance are extended to all of God's daughters, the one woman to whom Jesus is closest seemingly is dismissed—his own mother. While Mary had the most pivotal role in his life from his conception to the start of his ministry, later words push her away. He had been making radical statements about family relationships: "If you love your father or mother more than you love me, you are not worthy of being mine" (Matthew 10:37).

> What could you expect from the twelve-year-old kid who had excused his three-day absence during a Passover trip with "Didn't you know that I must be in my Father's house?" Maybe being a little too dedicated to learning and engaging in his faith traditions could be called precocious, leaving Mary to "[store] all these things in her heart" (Luke 2:49, 51).

But lately his teaching had gone too far to the edge—a source of real concern for his family. He was challenged by some Pharisees one day because his hungry disciples had picked grain to eat on a Sabbath day. In a verbal tussle, Jesus again demonstrated the holes in their legalism, and then declared, "The Son of Man is Lord, even over the Sabbath" (Luke 6:5). So he elevated himself to the point of being over the law. Then he declared, "It is right to do good on the Sabbath" and healed a man with a deformed hand right outside a synagogue of all places. The Pharisees knew how he was eroding their power, even if at times he sounded deranged, and it was time to talk about how to eliminate him (Matthew 12:1–14). It didn't take much to sense how Jesus was inviting trouble that maybe he didn't need.

That trouble went so far that his mother along with his brothers showed up. The family dynamics must have been tense by then. When told they wanted to talk with him, Jesus rebuffed even his own kin. "Who is my mother? Who are my brothers?" Pointing to his disciples, he declared, "Anyone who does the will of my Father in heaven is my brother and sister and mother!" (vv. 46–50).

> What's with this guy? He wants a fight with his own family? Relationships are what he's supposed to be about. Where is the loving, forgiving, healing figure that gave hope to the hopeless?

The answer likely lies in his response to another woman who calls out to him, "God bless your mother—the womb from which you came, and the breasts that nursed you!" While at least he doesn't take away from these words, he just can't leave it there, replying, "But even more blessed are all who hear the word of God and put it into practice" (Luke 11:27–28). No one, no matter how dear a person may be, is deemed more important or precious than the work of God brought into flesh by the Son of God to reverse and restore humanity to their God.

> Dear, dear Jesus. On the one hand, you reverse some of the lowest of our kind. The sick, the sinners, the saintly who yearn to learn from you and wipe their hair with their tears on your feet are given your mercy, grace, and love. But then your own mother you turn away? Why, in God's name, do you never address her as mother, only as woman, like she is no more to you than any other?

Or is that it? She is no more than any other daughter, but all women are no less than she, blessed in being given access to Jesus in person, spirit, and service for him, called to uphold the law in love. May they know and be worthy of who Jesus is through their creation as females.

Women, undervalued at best, mostly disregarded, frequently abused by their closest relationships as well as their religion, knew trouble of their own. In following Jesus, however, they found affirmation in the wholeness of their creation and knew the love of God. Yet, though Jesus reversed their trouble, these women accepted upon themselves *his* trouble, becoming the most faithful among his followers when the worst would come.

From their place of powerlessness, they could do nothing to defend him as the political and religious forces combined to twist sentiment against him. Yet, as their male counterparts, particularly the disciples, deserted and fled when he was falsely tried, sentenced, and led to the cross, women fought their fear and grief, staying near, brave both by presence and devotion, faithful until his last breath (Matthew 27:55–56; Mark 15:40–41; Luke 23:49; John 19:25–27). They could not stop or fight against the grisly horror before them, but they couldn't succumb to the shock of it either. Theirs would be the final gift and honor given to their Lord. Those women whom Jesus did not forsake did not forsake him as he died.

Though sunset brought Sabbath rest, quiet, refraining from labor, some women worked quickly to gather the necessary ointments and spices for his embalming. They had followed as his lifeless body was taken down from his final seat of trouble, his bloody cross. Watching as he was laid in a nearby tomb, they knew it was sealed with a great rock and guarded by Roman sentinels. Still, they resolved to bring a final anointing to the one who had given them new life and eternal life. Before the dawn of light that first day of the week, they met with their gifts of love at his resting place (Mark 15:46–47; Luke 23:55–56).

Now what follows, though not as significant in any way to the miracle of death being reversed into life in Jesus's resurrection, is still monumental. Yet typically it's not frequently related, at least with the import and emphasis it should receive. All four of the Gospel records state it. When Jesus rose from the dead, it was to women that angels declared he lived, it was to women that he first appeared, and it was women who carried the good news to the disciples and thus to the world (Matthew 28:1–10; Mark 16:1–10; Luke 24:1–10; John 20:1–2, 11–18). Their grief reversed into full joy, their mourning knew celebration, their hope was fulfilled. He was alive!

There was also that woman Jesus did call by name. Outside the garden tomb on that day after the Sabbath, Mary Magdalene discovered Jesus's grave empty and ran to find Peter and John. Then the men saw for themselves the great stone rolled away and the folded burial linen cloths lying within. While astonished, even as the realization of resurrection was setting in, they still did not meet Jesus there. Women would be the first to meet him again (John 20:14–18). The announcement of Jesus's resurrection and his appearance to Mary Magdalene accomplished another reversal started by that woman in the first garden who misunderstood a lie, "You won't die!" (Genesis 3:4). Now Jesus's love and grace, first extended to women, would be for all to live eternally.

"Mary" (John 20:16). No one spoke her name as he did. Jesus told her to bring the good news to his disciple brothers. She runs to exclaim, "I have seen the Lord!" (v. 18). With the good news given first to Mary Magdalene, trouble becomes triumph.

Further Provocations for Your Consideration

1. "No one must have wanted a Messiah more than a woman." In today's society, the oppression of women is not wrapped around any regulation of their monthly periods. Still, even with progressive changes, how and where do women find themselves limited and without power over their lives and futures? What is Jesus offering to women and those termed as "other"?

_____

_____

_____

_____

2. "Yet it was because of his ministry to women that he also upset the status quo. The value he ascribed to women created a trajectory of freedom in rights to be ascribed to all persons. In doing so, he also set the bar high for moral standards." Linked with Jesus's upset of traditional roles of gender and affirmations of women is a higher calling for relationships, particularly in marriage. How is this surprising? In what ways is it necessary for both to occur together?

_____

_____

_____

_____

_____

3. Women were the first to be told of Jesus's resurrection and the first to carry the message to others. Shepherds, people who lived and worked on the fringes, were the first to hear of Jesus's birth and to carry that message. What is the common thread in these stories? What implications does it have in understanding Jesus's life and who God is?

_____

_____

_____

_____

_____

_____

5

His Teachings Threw Curves

They had been on the edges for much of the time, not being drawn in fully but not going away either, caught in their thoughts. By now they found themselves drawn to this teacher who was not afraid to challenge the religious leaders who were keeping a close eye on him as well as on them. Even so, they stayed back for much of the time, knowing he was dangerous to them as well. For at the core of his message was change, reversal, a way of upsetting how they understood and looked at life. No shallow meaning or easy answers could explain him otherwise.

Unsure of what they thought of him, the uncommitted kept arms across their chests, faces unexpressive as they listened intensely to Jesus's teaching.

Ok, Jesus, we get where you stand on most things, and we kind of like it. You give everybody a fair chance. You see a person beyond the usual places of education, status, heritage, even gender. That's something we've grown up with, what we've learned about how the world works, but you want better for us. You walk a fine line with those ideas. But with all those you've attracted close to you, you'll probably get away with some of it, especially given how you couch your message and call on your hearers to receive it like children. There's not much threat in that, and as long as the priests and Roman guards still get their cut in the deal, paying the temple and the tax, this might not be so bad.

Except there's that stuff on money. Now that's moving more to an edge. You really think people with money are going to just drop cash from the trees for the benefit of an average guy? Zacchaeus started out in a tree and bought your story, but face it, he was so out there, no real friends and hated so much. Wasn't he just buying popularity? You kicked in some guarantee of heaven with his newfound generosity, so he really made out well then.

See, your preaching, teaching, whatever you want to call it, just doesn't seem to fly in the real world. Maybe you should come at this in a different way. Otherwise, we're walking away, and all you'd be left with is a gang that's out for you and no one to hold them back.

You're right. Standing on a mountain and proclaiming blessing followed by radical statements might not be the best approach for assembling a following. His tactic is instructive, and Jesus certainly speaks with an authority the people haven't known before, but maybe after a while, his message becomes too didactic. People don't like being told what to do all the time: what's right, what's wrong, what he says is the best way to get into the kingdom of God. Sometimes, it's better to let them figure it out for themselves, do the spiritual wrestling in their own thoughts or when they meet later in private gatherings. Then they can take what he says or leave it. But for those who do get him, the truth and power of his message lasts.

He's a little slow at first, almost just tagging short illustrations on at the end of his talks, but the impact doesn't go away. Those who stay on the sides of crowds or against the walls of little rooms begin to hear stories that relate to life as they know it, the moral dilemmas people find themselves in, the greater questions of life's meaning. The universality of the narratives goes deep, leaving the hearer not with all the answers at once. Their meanings knock around in the soul with Jesus's aim of reversing, redirecting what one has been taught to believe. That's as dangerous as you can make it, and where the trouble ultimately lies.

Who Is My Neighbor?

The man who stood up on one of these days of listening to the rogue rabbi from Nazareth was bold and clever. Brilliant in religious law, he was shrewd in his question. It was a valid one, a basic yet high moral query which delineates where one sits on theological spectrums. "Teacher," he addresses him, "What should I do to inherit eternal life?" (Luke 10:25). Those around him knew they were in for a really interesting exchange. Clearly, it was a test. Could Jesus hold his own in this verbal confrontation? If not, things were going to get dangerous. The threat was underplayed but noticeable.

Oh, Jesus was smart though. All good cross-examinations should have the opportunity for clarity. So Jesus throws it back to him. "What does the law of Moses say? How do you read it?" (v. 26). Okay, counselor, let's start on common ground. We're both Jews. What would any good Jew tell you about it?

The lawyer is succinct and goes straight to the Torah with no problem: "'You must love the Lord your God with all your heart, all your soul, all your strength, and all your mind.' And, 'Love your neighbor as yourself'" (v. 27; Deuteronomy 6:5; Leviticus 19:18).

A perfect answer gets the perfect response: "Right!" The great commandment still holds weight with the teacher. "Do this and you will live!" (Luke 10:28).

Isn't that what the lawyer wanted to hear? Likely not, for he pressed on, asking a question that not only would define terms for his legalistic mindset but also reveal his own issues in relationship: "And who is my neighbor?" (v. 29). Loving one's family and friends would be the logical answer. Love those who are yours, those with whom you have built close relationships of support. The trouble with Jesus was he consistently pushed out the expected parameters of love.

In asking the question, the lawyer asked for something that cut the law down to a manageable size rather than seeming generalities. Doing so also would set up the real test for Jesus in the questioning. If Jesus responded as if he knew better than the lawyer, he was playing with fire, threatening those who would have him removed quickly. His answer had to be one that would give the lawyer a pause, something to consider that was beyond the standard examination of the religious leaders. Jesus needed to be able to walk away for the time being and leave them not knowing what hit them.

Rather than giving him a lawbook answer, Jesus astutely changed tactics. Instead of a sermon or engaging in an outright argument, he told a story, a parable with the unique quality of teaching a lesson on life. In doing so, he turned the story back on the lawyer with his own brand of character test. Jesus's response is known throughout the world as the parable of the good Samaritan.

"A Jewish man was traveling from Jerusalem down to Jericho, and he was attacked by bandits. They stripped him of his clothes, beat him up, and left him half dead beside the road" (v. 30).

Who is my neighbor? This isn't anyone I know—just a guy in the wrong place at the wrong time. What's my responsibility to him? The moral question is posed. The key detail in the situation that Jesus gives is that the victim is Jewish. You may not have known him in any other way except he is just like the lawyer and everyone else listening. He's one of them. He comes from the same heritage and faith that they do. He's a brother descended from Abraham. They are the chosen people, and so is he. Beaten and robbed, his situation is dire; he's going to need help and need it soon. Who is my neighbor? He is.

Maybe so, but it's not enough. Jesus continued the story, and it doesn't look good for his audience. A priest and a Levite who worked as a temple assistant come by on the same road. Both clearly see the man, beaten and bleeding, lying there. The man is one of them, kin not so far removed from those gathered around. Likewise, the lawyer also represents people like the religious authorities—the priests and Levites who frequent the synagogues and often serve near or in the temple. All are Jews, just like the man who needs help in the worst way and soon. But as it is, his brothers pass by on the other side of the road.

Their actions are understandable, and all those hearing this story knew why. It wasn't a matter of simple inconvenience or delay in their travel. It wasn't only that by stopping to help they could be opening themselves to the same danger this guy had experienced. If these two men had stopped to help, it would have been more than messy. With all his injuries that put him near death, the man's body had been crushed, smashed into a bloody pulp. And therein lies the problem: exposure and contact with blood would make any who touched him, helped him in any way, ceremonially unclean by their own ritualistic law. That meant a minimum of seven days of isolation from family and friends and their most important jobs. Whatever sense of pity they may have felt, however they may have prayed for this guy, their positions made it difficult for them to intervene and help. So they walked around the poor soul and did nothing for him. "Love your neighbor" was just not their call. Once again Jesus did not endear these status-sensitive religious bosses to the populace.

Jesus, is that it? You're saying to leave this guy who'd been mugged to a deadly fate that is ignored, no help in sight? Is loving my neighbor to mean stick together in your own pack and just take care of your own? You sound just like they do.

> Who needs this! Life really is a crap shoot, and even messiahs
> won't roll the dice in our favor.

To this fictional scenario, Jesus provided an ending that ends well, but it's an ending that slams everyone there, regardless of rank, prominence, or class. The man finally gets the help he needs, but it comes from an unlikely and despised source—a Samaritan. Not only does the Samaritan dress his wounds and take him to an inn to recover, but he also personally takes care of the man and pays the innkeeper extra for his care with a promise of more the next time the Samaritan came through that area. He does the right thing and cares for his neighbor as God would have any who follow his law do so.

> Good for him! And good for you, Jesus! You both passed
> that test and put that law-loving solicitor in his place. We get
> what you're doing here. You're letting the fat guys know what
> we think of their rules, and God's will still gets done. Hey, we
> can go with this kind of thing. Give us more.

More is what all of them get. It was now Jesus's turn to ask a question, a follow-up to "who is my neighbor?" And in doing so, he threw the lawyer's question 180 degrees in another direction. "Now which of these three would you say was a neighbor to the man who was attacked by bandits?" (Luke 10:36). Who is my neighbor gets a turnaround, a reversal of the original question. In Jesus's question, "neighbor" no longer means the one who is in need.

The crowd was stunned. These people were all Jews, and Jews hated Samaritans for all the racial, ethnic, and religious reasons that the human race can dig up to separate one person from another. In other words, what slammed Jesus's listeners was that their despised enemy was really the one acting neighborly and thus whom then they should love if they were to obey God's commandment. It was another way of saying what Jesus had instructed in that sermon on the mount in Matthew 5:43–45, "You have heard the law that says, 'Love your neighbor' and hate your enemy. But I say, love your enemies! Pray for those who persecute you! In that way, you will be acting as true children of your Father in heaven."

The lawyer was forced to answer Jesus's question. It was a question that didn't allow for an ending that made him or the audience feel good about what happened. For they realized Jesus is calling them to love those whom they didn't want to love, the ones they had been taught to despise and hate for generations. Their enemy was now their neighbor, and if they were to follow the law to "love your neighbor as yourself," if they were to receive eternal life, they had to reverse and change all their relationships. The lawyer replied with the "correct" answer, the one that would get him out of the test he started. "The one who showed him mercy" (Luke 10:37). The loathed Samaritan was the neighbor to the one in need. The lawyer must grant that. But he would not use the word "Samaritan." Instead, he just referred to him as "the one."

Jesus, then, held the lawyer to the fire. If he wanted eternal life, Jesus told him, "Yes, now go and do the same" (v. 37). Do what the Samaritan did! Do what your enemy did!

> Well, that's a different take on an old tale. Being a good Samaritan is a lot more than helping out some poor guy on the road. If people did this, loved those who were not like them, barriers of race and ethnicity would fall faster than a thousand-pound anchor to the ocean floor. People can wrap their minds around this kind of teaching. So what happened next?

Just what you think would happen. He even said it: "For all that is secret will eventually be brought into the open, and everything that is concealed will be brought to light and made known to all. So pay attention to how you hear. To those who listen to my teaching, more understanding will be given. But for those who are not listening, even what they think they understand will be taken away from them" (8:17–18). To heed the true meaning of loving our neighbor is revolutionary in comparison to how the world works. The response more often has been to dilute the story into what it is not: see a need; meet that need. That's an easier take on the parable and will make you even feel good about fulfilling it. But to be in relationship and service alongside your enemy is a whole other take. Jesus knew there were those who were listening. And there were those who listened but didn't like what they heard. The trouble was, Jesus kept at it.

The Lost and the Found

Frequently when Jesus taught, those of ill repute were in the crowd, such as tax collectors and "other notorious sinners" (15:1). Usually, it wasn't your Sunday school picnic assemblage. The religionist marshals took note. With no intent of being helpful to this gifted rabbi, they complained. He was seen getting a little too close to the scum, even eating and drinking with them, the winos and gluttons that they were. Reputations are made by who your friends are. So why did Jesus seem to prefer, maybe even have a better time with, the likes of these?

He answers with three parables about things that were lost. In each one, something has gone missing but is recovered. The first two are easy to swallow. A sheep wandered from the fold. Even though there are ninety-nine already safe in the pen, the shepherd goes out into the wilderness and searches. This shepherd finds the lost animal and carries it home securely on his shoulders. He then invites friends and neighbors to rejoice, to be happy with him that the animal is safe and back in the fold (vv. 3–7).

Similarly, a woman lost a coin, understood in that culture to be part of her wedding dowry. Even though she already had nine other coins, she searched diligently in every nook and cranny of her house until she found the lost one. Having done so, she also shared her joy with her neighbors (vv. 8–10).

> Nice job, Jesus! Somebody should stretch this into a spiritual song about once lost but now found. Okay, already done. But we get the point. God loves even little lost sheep, so to speak, seeing those who are lost as having inherent value, like a coin. God doesn't want to let even one get away. That's love. That's compassion. We all need more of that. You see, make your religion all about altruistic inclusive efforts, and you can get away with those late-night parties with your low-life friends. Yeah, this works just fine.

Perhaps Jesus knew this would happen, how his message would get bent, slanted into what people want to hear. People need small doses sometimes. Break the lesson up into parts, giving a little more as you go along. So there's a follow-up parable, this one known best as The Prodigal Son. Everyone likes this one.

"A man had two sons . . ." You know what's coming. It's familiar, a story about family. Families are hotbeds of conflict, so this is going to be a good tale. Jesus got straight to it.

The younger of the two sons wants his share of his inheritance from his father's estate now.

> Now? Before his dad has kicked the bucket? That's bold. What's the deal? Does he feel his old man doesn't know how to invest his money well and wants to take over?

If only the kid had that much sense, but don't think so highly of him. Remember as well, demanding one's inheritance like this just wasn't done in Jesus's day and age. It spoke clearly of the disrespect the younger son had for his father and what he had achieved in life. Right away, the crowd's estimation of the jerk was sliding down fast. But dad caves to him, giving the kid what he wants.

Sure enough, a few days later, the ingrate takes off. Jesus said the son headed for "a distant land" (v. 13), as far away from his father's home and influence as he could get. Soon Jesus will make that lost sheep story look like a sweet little children's story. Every parent's heart is picking up in beats at this point. Worst fears are going to be realized. The spoiled brat doesn't disappoint. "He wasted all his money in wild living," Jesus delicately put it (v. 14). There have been enough renditions of this story to know what that means, and high moral living isn't a part of it.

Don't worry. The prodigal got his due. Just as his money ran out, there was an economic downturn, so to speak, a famine. Before long, this good-for-nothing was literally starving. For maybe the first time in his life, he had to do some real work. A person's empty belly can be a real motivator. But the only job he could get was feeding pigs, and even then, pig slop looked appetizing to him.

> Disgusting! Weren't pork rind and other swine products off limits, unclean foods the law called them? Well, this shows it. You reap what you sow. Tough lesson, but it happens.

Calm down. This parable is longer than the other lost stories, and the pattern is for the lost to be found. In this case, though, there is the one lost in the wilderness of wild living and another living in a lostness of his own. Right now, however, the wastrel is sitting in a pigsty, abandoned to his hunger and fate.

Hitting bottom is where some people land when they have made choices with consequences that are extremely negative. As bad as things are, some people will still sit in the pigsty and stay there, sinking farther down, until they are looking up at what had been the bottom. Note how the wayward son is unnamed, but in telling this story, Jesus has given meaning to "prodigal." This son is lost. He needs to be found. However, in this story no one goes searching for him. The narrative curves differently from what happens with sheep and coins.

Referring again to the prodigal son, Jesus says, "When he finally came to his senses" (v. 17). No one has shown up to take him home. No one rescues him, saying, *It's all right. We'll take care of you, shouldering you above the mess you've made.* In the muck and filth of pigs, out of the deep sucking mud, rising from the stench of his own skin, comes a realization that would not have enlightened his mind otherwise. He finally came to his senses. Reversing his thoughts, desires, even his needs, now repentant of what he has done, the pitiful young man makes a decision. He will return home to his dad, confess his sin of wronging his sacred relationships with the two who gave him life, his father and God, and his unworthiness before both. "Please take me on as a hired servant," he will ask his father (v. 19). Less than son, relinquishing control of his life and only asking for a meager existence, he pulls himself away from where he thought the "good life" would lead and starts the painful journey of regret back home.

What he didn't know as he trudged along the path that had led to his destitution was that his father spotted him "while he was still a long way off" (v. 20). Perhaps this father had often looked down this road remembering when his boy had left, run off really, forsaking all the lessons and love that he had received from his father. Now, in the space of distance and time between them, the father saw a different man, one defeated by the choices he had made, desperate for only a chance to survive. But more importantly, the father also saw his son was coming home. Whatever had separated them would be restored.

Driven by love and compassion, the father runs to meet his prodigal son, catching him in an embrace that dissolves all separation. Is this a good thing?

Well, it is more than generous of the dad. He could have kicked his son back into the next pigpen, which is what the kid deserved anyway. Evidently, the love of this father had never changed. He had hoped and prayed this day would come—the day when he could have his son back. I guess the question is if this is a good thing for their relationship. People do a lot of bad things and will do anything to get out of their mess. Is the dad just setting himself up for more hurt later on down the road?

Smart. No one is blaming the dad for his love he still has for the son. But love alone won't do it. While the son knows he has done wrong, it has to be expressed, admitted, sealed between them what has happened. The son confesses how he disregarded the sacred relationship of son to father and how that also violated his relationship with God. Herein is also a difference from when he sat in the pigsty. Unlike before, he doesn't ask for what he wants. He doesn't ask to be taken on even as a hired hand or servant to the father. He leaves that judgment to the father. He has come to his senses one more time. He cannot control what the father will do but only trust there will be mercy (v. 21).

And there is. Not just acceptance and forgiveness, but extravagant mercy, undeserved in the measure it is given. In his joy, the father calls for a fine robe, sandals, and a ring to dress his son, covering him again as beloved son. As in the other parables, there is celebration and plans for a great feast. "'This son of mine was dead and has now returned to life. He was lost, but now he is found.' So the party began" (v. 24).

The son was dead to what he was, now returned to a new life. He was lost in who he was, now found in what he has become. Reversal brings joyful restoration and more, celebration in heaven over repentance and returning to God.

"Meanwhile, the older son . . ." (v. 25). Here this third parable takes a turn unlike the other two. The party is in full swing. Food, dancing, laughter, and lots of "welcome home" for the wayward son who has rejoined his family. But the older son doesn't get what was going on. He had always been the good child, the one who met all expectations, bringing honor to his father unlike his kid brother. Even that day, he had been out in the fields, overseeing his father's workers and minding the family business. Finding a midday, midweek party going on was the last thing he expected as he comes home. He doesn't take this well. He refuses to go inside the house and take part in the festivities.

When his father hears his older son is hovering outside, he goes out to talk with him.

> Seems like this dad is always going out to look for his boys. Chasing kids is his full-time job.

Good point.

Big brother explodes on the dad. For years, he'd been the one who stayed, not the slacker like his brother. For years, he followed orders, doing everything according to his father's wishes. Did he ever get a big party? No, not once. But now his kid brother gets an all-day fiesta with filet mignon as the main course.

> This for the guy who'd taken the family wealth and thrown it away on wild women and that kind of lifestyle? It wasn't right, just not fair. What kind of father would do this?

That depends. What are you looking for here? Justice? Due reward? You think "reap what you sow" should be the primary principle for the younger son? Turning back, repentance, means nothing in that kind of world. Lock him into that pigpen and throw away the key. It's what he deserves.

Interesting, isn't it? The son who had stayed the closest to his father may have been the son who was as far away from his dad's heart as you can get, just as lost as his brother. The younger son, even as he sat among the pigs, knew his father's generous, unending love. He knew no matter how far the distance between them, he could always go home. The older one, the one who in his faithfulness had never strayed away, never saw it, never realized how much his father had missed and grieved the lost son. More significantly, he didn't feel or share that loss with his father. All he saw in his brother's return was what he didn't get—a party, a one-day hoopla and time off from work.

Dad knows and reassures him of his love. Their relationship will not change. The younger son has spent his inheritance while the older son also received his inheritance, actually what amounted to two-thirds of their father's estate (Deuteronomy 21:17). That's fair. Yet, the father also explains what this day meant. All that time, the father had felt and feared the worst: *Will my son ever return home? Is he even still alive?* Now, however, his son had come back and gained a new life. So as in the other narratives, the lost had been found.

Okay, so that's it? What did big brother do? How did he answer his father? Did he join the party and welcome his brother, or did he pack his bags and take off himself?

Jesus doesn't say. He leaves it there. He doesn't tell us what the older son chose to do. Was his father's answer to him enough, or did the older son remain in his anger and sense of injustice? What do you think?

The abrupt ending without tying up loose ends is deliberate. Nearby, both the "notorious sinners" and the religious elite heard the stories. It was pretty obvious where the tax collectors and their kind fit in. Lost sheep, lost coins, lost sons were of their kind. But this older son character was the stickler. He had followed the rules. He stayed pure. Yes, as the older son he would receive the greater share of his father's inheritance. Yet what he hadn't learned was the breadth of his father's love, how it extended to and included his problem child, how his heart was broken over the younger son's choices. Even with all the hurt the prodigal had caused, the father had watched and waited for him to come to his senses and come home. With the act of turning back, mercy and forgiveness were activated. Love was centered in grace. For this, heaven threw a party.

The prodigals and the pious all heard the story. Both knew what was available to them. Would the lost ones return? Would those who had stayed in the sheep fold of the synagogue rejoice when the sinners came back home? Could they see how desirable and valued both were, how God would search, watch, receive, and rejoice over them all? Jesus left the final scene of the narrative open for them to tell their own story.

> Nice touch there. Not a sermon, do-this-or-else kind of holy-hell threat. Just put it out there, let them know where God stands, let people come to their senses on their own. Even so, does this mean you can get away with anything? Take off, have a good time. Do like the rich guy did. Eat, drink, be merry, and when it all falls apart, just go home with your tail between your legs. God has this covered.

One doesn't have to read the Bible to understand you reap what you sow is still operational. People are behavioral. Freedom to make choices is God-given. Choices have consequences. But once made, consequences can sometimes choose the unintended for you. You'd think people would make choices that have positive consequences. Yet some of them are slow learners and take longer. Are you going to be mad at God for that?

What's Due and Extravagance

Jesus had another story, this one that has the holy houses still talking. It's got all the elements of reap what you sow, and he throws in money just to make sure people pay attention. Calm down, though. This time, it's not about the money.

The owner of an estate early one morning hired workers for his vineyard. He agreed to pay them the going rate for a day's work. At 9 a.m., he ran into some guys in the marketplace who had not been hired that day. He hired them and promised to make it good at the end of the day. At noon and at 3 p.m., he did the same with more workers. Finally, at 5 p.m. some more guys were standing around. They told the estate owner no one had hired them that day. He told them to join the other workers in the vineyard.

Evening came, and the owner told his foreman to pay all the workers, starting with those who were hired last. The five-o-clockers got a full day's wage. Those hired earlier in the day assumed they would get more for having worked longer. But they were paid just a full day's wage too, no more than the last guys who had only worked an hour or so (Matthew 20:1–12).

> Really? The guys who sweated all day got no more than the ones who didn't show up until most of the work was done and barely did a thing? Jesus, this would not go over well with corporations or the unions. You pay for work performed. Reap what you sow, remember? You get out what you put in. That's how fairness is played.

The owner doesn't see it that way. He contracted with the early shift to pay the full day's wage. They agreed. The ink was dry, and the papers sealed. The owner argued there was no law saying he couldn't pay out whatever he wanted to whomever he wanted regardless of when they clocked in because, after all, it was his money (vv. 13–14). Then he really needled them. "Should you be jealous because I am kind to others?" (v. 15).

Oh, for crying out loud, this isn't about kindness. It's about fairness. Everyone should be treated equally. Justice is at the core of this. You don't reward someone for getting to the table late. You're talking about people's wallets here. Give a guy what he's due.

You don't really mean that. Rather, you really don't want that. For if you hold that measure of rule up for one, it won't go well for all. Go back a minute. The Samaritan saved a guy's life, not the priest or the Levite. If you want a system of reward the good and leave out the bad, should the ones who left a hurt and bleeding man on the side of the road get their due? Jesus never says anything like that. Then, too, the younger son, bad as he was, repented and came back home, while his brother was jealous and angry about a little celebration his father gave. Should the one with a cold heart be disowned? So here, too, the owner made his deal. Everyone got paid the same. Are you going to lay some system of fairness on him when it's his game to begin with? You don't like his kindness and generosity. If the shoe was on the other foot, though, how loud would your protest be?

Issues of justice are significant. The poor should not be exploited and ripped off for what little they have. Blessings of wealth are to be shared. Women are not to be subjected to practices that isolate just because of natural biological functions. High standards of living and relationship are required for all. No question there.

Yet the flip side of justice is grace. Everyone is a slow learner in some way, everyone wanders off at some time, and some run as far as they can get. Extending grace doesn't negate what's right. Instead, it's based on the extravagant grace God loves to give. And that grace is given out to everyone, whether they ignore the right thing to do, get lost and have a hard time getting home, or show up for work really late. When love is received, especially when it's love that can cost the giver a lot more than what would generally be fair, it settles in the soul bringing reversals and transformations not otherwise possible. That change is seen best by those who would allow grace in the lives of others.

Jesus said, "Those who are last now will be first then, and those who are first will be last" (v. 16). His message asserts that those who assume they have it all together with God may be last in heaven's estimation. Likewise, those who feel unworthy of coming home are the ones for whom parties are thrown. His parable stories throw a calculated curve on how the world thinks life works. For some, his message is restorative. For others, it is threatening and spells trouble.

Further Provocations for Your Consideration

1. The parable of the good Samaritan is classic. What was your understanding of the story? Has it changed? How is loving your enemy part of loving your neighbor?

_____

_____

_____

_____

_____

_____

_____

_____

_____

_____

2. Likewise, stories of lost sheep, coins, and sons are famous. Why would these stories be problematic for the well-established and privileged? What is the connection to these parables and the one about the good Samaritan?

_____

_____

_____

_____

_____

_____

3. How do justice and grace collide in the narrative of the vineyard owner and his workers? Why do you think that Jesus uses an example based in monetary rewards for this story? Would this parable be saying that all who come back to the Father in repentance get the same reward as those who have always been with the ninety-nine in the sheepfold? If so, how is this understanding problematic for some people?

_____

_____

_____

_____

_____

_____

4. Jesus takes the everyday and familiar and diverts it into layers of unexpected meaning as he tells these stories. Is this troublesome when well-established beliefs are considered? What makes his approach so effective?

_____

_____

_____

_____

_____

_____

_____

_____

_____

_____

6

He Refused to Be
The Divine Fixer

"**C**an anything good come from Nazareth?" (John 1:46). The crowd has been watching this troublemaker and has seen reversals that only upset and disturb the way the world works. They are equally disturbed.

> Not surprised, Jesus, not surprised. The best you can surround yourself is with low-life followers and women who cater to you? Then you want people's money for your plan of helping those who have no use in the world? Good God, what is this! Your stories portray nice philosophies, but can't you do anything that at least makes everyone's life better?

Without power and position to support him, Jesus the Nazarene set standards of relationship, money, and morals that were outside the tendencies, desires, and standards of the first-century culture. It was in his ministry to those who would follow him—women, disciples with low personal status, tax collectors, the poor, and the reformed rich—that forgiveness and grace were extended by truly denying one's personal self, one's own ambitions and desires. By his outrageous claim of authority as the Son of God, Jesus threatened those who claimed religious and political power. Even so, his messianic assertions would have been completely discounted if not for the signs revealed in his miracles—great reversals of the natural processes of illness, disease, and even death.

The prophet John the Baptist called Jesus the "Chosen One," the one upon whom the Holy Spirit had descended like a dove at his baptism (v. 34). Almost immediately, Jesus went to the desert to spiritually wrestle with what this would mean, and he had that face-to-face confrontation with his antithesis and antagonist, the devil, who would have him stop the story before it even got started. However, these were internal spiritual experiences, not part of the witnessed drama staged for all time. To fulfill his destiny as Savior of the world, Jesus had to demonstrate a power that pointed to him as one not just from God but as God incarnate, the Word made flesh, alive and deeply personal in the lives of those who would believe and follow him.

He had gathered a few followers, as most rabbis would. In the ensuing years, they would witness how miracles, reversals of the natural order, would become what the writer of the Gospel of John would call "signs"—that which point to Jesus not as a rabbinical teacher but as the Messiah. "Come and see," Jesus said. That is, come and learn from me, enter into understanding that gives not just sight to the blind but insight into the ways of God.

> Oh God, who wants that? Give me all for which I hunger, wish, crave, desire, and more, but don't change me. That means trouble.

Still, Jesus tried. He went to the synagogues and preached the good news. And wherever he went, he healed people of every sort of disease and illness: the paralyzed, epileptic, blind, mute, even those possessed with demons, those frightening, mysterious conditions that tortured the mind and soul. He had pity on the sufferers, for they were at the end of their ropes, not knowing where else to go for help, like sheep without a shepherd. These miraculous healings brought what is repeatedly called "multitudes" to hear his message. These who had been afflicted in life, those with no choice but to endure what life had dumped on them, now had hope.

But in the places where Jesus most often brought the miraculous, lives did not change. They would not know God, and therein lay his trouble. His compassion for those who could not improve their lives or help themselves was immense. Poverty in the first century likely involved as much as 70 percent of the population. Food insecurity, lack of clean water, and disease contributed as much as unjust oppression and unfair pressure from both political and religious leaders. Even though his miracles reversed people's immediate suffering, most people were not interested in turning their lives around to honor God by loving their enemy as well as their neighbor, sharing the blessings of wealth, seeing in the lowly those whom God loved. He heard the grumbling then as is now: *Who wants that?* And did Jesus ever take notice of it.

A Little Gratitude

He was just entering a village when ten lepers, standing away at a good distance, cried out to him: "Jesus, Master, have mercy on us!" (Luke 17:13). Mercy certainly was what they needed. Leprosy was strictly regulated by Jewish law. Besides being a dreadful, life-altering physical disease, it carried much shame. Persons so afflicted were required to shout "Unclean!" to any who approached. Judgment hung heavy over those living with it based on the thinking that persons had brought it upon themselves. Besides no cure being available in the first-century world, the social isolation it brought on was devastating to all familial and social relationships. Enormous stigma surrounded this disease, and for the large part, leprosy was considered a death sentence.

Embedded in this story is confirmation of what helped so many to survive throughout the centuries. Disease can be a great leveler. Lepers of varying social status, wealth, age, race, and gender would form a kind of colony, leaning on each other for survival of their common misery. This particular group of leprous men, mostly Jewish, had among them a Samaritan. Remember, Jews hated Samaritans for all the religious, ethnic, racial prejudices people can drag up. But in this little tribe, there was no discriminating when all shared a commonality of scabs, sores, and numbness in the extremities.

Jesus "looked at them" (v. 14). Get that? He looked at them—that is, he saw them as they were, ten men who dearly needed the mercy for which they cried, mercy which would restore them not only from physical affliction but also from the loneliness, the separateness, and the rejection that kept them apart from others who could love, work, and worship together.

The great compassion for which Jesus was known was put into play before anyone could even tell. "Go show yourselves to the priests," he told them (v. 14). The law required they had to be certified as "clean" to be approved as cured so that they could return to their lives. But the most miraculous thing was, as they were on their way, the leprosy disappeared (v. 14). Scales fell, skin became full and firm, fingers and toes tingled in sensation. Who wouldn't run off in joy and excitement?

Take note: for whatever reason, nine of the now healed lepers never gave so much as a "Yea, God" for how they'd been cured. They just ran off. What does that tell you about what people want from their God?

Children have to be taught to say thank you when someone does something nice for them. These healed lepers were adults. Did they still need to be taught? Had they learned to be grateful? Or were they so hardened within that words of gratitude couldn't even pass their lips, even after being healed of such a dreaded disease?

Uh, excuse me, but Jesus, let's extend a little grace here, okay? Maybe these men were just overwhelmed, swept up with what had happened to them. Maybe they just plain forgot. Perhaps it was carelessness from having not been trained as children to say thank you when someone does something nice for you. Give the guys a break, okay?

Sure. Or it very well could be that they were just plain ungrateful. All of this is hard to believe given what they had been through and how they found themselves healed. But from where Jesus stood, only dust rose to heaven from their running feet.

Except…one of the healed men did turn back. Of all of them, the one who returned to Jesus was the Samaritan, the despised one, the enemy of the Jews. His dreaded skin disease was gone, but he would still know the prejudice and outright hatred for being who he was and to whom he was born. That aspect of his life would not change regardless of any approval by a priest that he was now "clean." He would never be accepted by them, maybe more so because of the disease he had shared with them. That circumstance would never change.

Still, he was the only one who turned back, praising God for this incredible change in his life. It meant so much he went back to worship and fell prostate at Jesus's feet. Jesus dryly notes: "Has no one returned to give glory to God except this foreigner?" (v. 18). Surely, it was a rhetorical question. Jesus had come not to those who required just a fixing of their circumstance. That wasn't his mission. Yet isn't that what happens when people practice thanksgiving? They express their happiness in what is good around them, such as nature and the heavens, one's very existence, good harvest, health, prosperity, victory in battle, and family. If the situation is good, they give thanks. When life is not good, they still search for the silver lining in the cloud. It's their state of affairs for which they show appreciation.

Still, only this foreigner returned. A foreigner this time, but in other places it was a tax collector, a prostitute, a fisherman, a desperate father, or a widowed mother. No matter what their circumstance, these models of faith understood best what Jesus had done for them. People know when they've been cured, but outcasts are the ones who know real, deep healing.

Jesus told the man, "Stand up and go" (v. 19). Stand, he said, rise up to the full stature of who you are in God's purpose. Go, move forward into life in that purpose. "Your faith has healed you" (v. 19). Your faith, your belief in your Healer as one who looked at you and welcomed you and met your need. To him, you were not an outsider, the disdained other, the one shunned more so because of your heritage than your health. Faith made the difference—that is, faith in the one who could heal him and did. It made this Samaritan well. It brought to him a full restoration that would not only deliver him from illness and isolation but that would also reconcile and restore him to God.

Based in circumstance, too often God is called upon to be The Divine Fixer. After that is granted, people tend to run off. That's what Jesus saw in the nine who were cured but didn't return to say thank you. Nevertheless, gratitude is deepest in those who have had lives reversed, who no longer see themselves as defined by others but as God sees them. Gratitude becomes boundless in who one will become by God's love and grace. God's greatest desire is gratitude for the life that is healed by Jesus.

Jesus keeps at it, though. He knows the people deserve better if only they could just realize and accept how he can reverse what oppresses them into what can give them life. That's not what they wanted, but these multitudes tracked and stalked his travels and location anyway. Some may have listened to his teachings, but there also is the sense that just as many, if not more, were there only to be cured of whatever ailed them. Between the two groups lay a third: those who just came in hopes of witnessing the spectacular. For all, Jesus had compassion both for their need and their misplaced motives. All this in the midst of the trouble that hovered around him.

Food for Thousands

For likely the first time in his life since he was a boy, Jesus made the decision not to attend the Passover festival. Jerusalem was dangerous for him. Jewish authorities were looking for him, knowing he would be teaching somewhere, maybe performing more of those healing miracles. But the crowds making their pilgrimage to Jerusalem's temple delayed their journey upon hearing that he was nearby. They sought him out mostly because of the healing stories.

After a long day of teaching and healing their sick, the time was late. Food had run out, and the crowd was as large as a village. The disciples urged him to send the people away for their own good, to find rest and nourishment, and just as much to give Jesus a break.

Jesus doesn't seem to understand. He tells them, "You give them something to eat" (Matthew 14:16 NIV). The disciples are tired with the day and weary with such a ridiculous statement. One of them, Andrew, points out that they only have five loaves of bread and two fish from a young boy's lunch. What good could that do for five thousand men, not counting the women and children?

It's almost as if Jesus totally ignored them or the reality of the situation. Asking the people to sit down, Jesus took the bread, blessed it, broke the bread, and gave it to the disciples to distribute. These four simple actions demonstrated gratefulness for provision from God. The result was that the multitude was fed until they were full. Incredibly, twelve baskets of leftover bread were gathered up afterward (vv. 18–21).

You sure? Sorry again, Jesus, but this one may stretch beyond the sensical. Can understand you need to reach all these people at once, but how do we know this wasn't just what you'd wanted? People finally reached into their sacks and started sharing what they had. Just proves there's more than enough to go around when equally, justly distributed. Don't try and make the situation splashier than it was.

(Deep breath here—in and out, like a prayer.) Consider this. This miracle of multiplication is the only miracle outside the resurrection that is included by each of the Gospel writers of Matthew, Mark, Luke, and John (Matthew 14:13–21; Mark 6:32–44; Luke 9:10–17; John 6:1–15). Possibly each writer included it in their account because it best exemplified what Jesus brought through demonstrating God's love by provision and how he was misunderstood in doing so. The same could be said today. But to include it consistently, with little variation, also says something—something like, it happened like this . . .

The Telling

If only his miracles could make it easy, an easy way to be followed and believed. Still, Jesus knew what was in people's hearts, distortions only leading to more trouble. Each time he healed the sick, fed the hungry, and brought life to the physically and spiritually dead, the possibility to be misunderstood and misinterpreted, pressed to be what others wanted for themselves rather than what God designed in a kingdom, would position him as a dangerous figure—one who would reverse cultural values and the status quo supported by those who held religious and political power. The stage is being set, the crowd stands ready to both cheer and cry out against him, and tensions build, all combining for the coming climax.

It is no surprise that sometimes when Jesus healed persons, he told them not to tell others about the source of their healing. Some commentators have said that it was a kind of reverse psychology ploy: tell people not to do something, and they can't wait to get right at it. Thus, the thinking goes, his healing miracles would go viral. However, even without such manipulations, the word was out, and crowds were coming in droves. Certainly, it cannot be denied that Jesus had compassion on these people who were without hope of otherwise being cured. They had no other recourse, and desperate people will do whatever they can.

One such person was another man with leprosy. His words to Jesus are telling: "If you are willing, you can heal me and make me clean" (Mark 1:40). He gave his disease and his life over to Jesus. *If you want to, if it's your will, Jesus, you can drastically change my situation.* The man's affliction, faith, acceptance for whatever measure of mercy possible, and kneeling posture all stirred pity, compassion, mercy in Jesus. It also must be noted that some early manuscripts of the story state Jesus was "moved with anger." At any rate, he touched the man saying, "I am willing. . . . Be healed!" (v. 3). Yet just as the man was instantly healed, Jesus also instructed him not to talk to anyone about his healing but to take his offering to the priest to be declared clean and healed. The guy couldn't help himself, however. He spread the news about his healing anyway (v. 45). You can't blame him for the relief and joy the healed man felt, but for Jesus the publicity was not so positive. Throngs surrounded him so much that he had to move out of town into secluded places. The crowds still found him, though, and they came from everywhere (v. 45).

Not That Food

The day following the feeding of the five thousand men plus women and children, and after some crazy boat trips chasing Jesus on the Sea of Galilee, the crowd catches up with him again. If Jerusalem was dangerous and needed to be avoided for now, these people brought another form of trouble.

Exhausted with all of it, Jesus tells them like it is. "I tell you the truth, you want to be with me because I fed you, not because you understood the miraculous signs" (John 6:26). They didn't get it. Bread blessed, broken, and given was not just to fill multitudinous bellies. Rather, it pointed to something else. It was a sign of the one whose power could bring them life in full, life beginning now and forever. "Spend your energy seeking the eternal life that the Son of Man can give you. For God the Father has given me the seal of his approval" (v. 27). *People, how much clearer can I be?*

They ask, "What should we do?" (v. 28). Maybe now, they were close to getting it. Maybe now, the healings had their intended affect. Maybe now, they would understand God's purpose in sending him to them. So Jesus answers: "This is the only work God wants from you: Believe in the one he has sent" (v. 29).

No, not now. "Show us a miraculous sign if you want us to believe in you. What can you do?" (v. 30).

What kind of Messiah do you want, people? After he fed them, Jesus had run for the hills. At that point he was so popular, they were ready to crown him their king. A king who had the power to make their lives better, better so they didn't have to be sick or hungry. They hadn't heard his words to the disciples, "You give them something to eat." They didn't understand that by using even what little resources available, the power of God is activated, and lives become full and purposeful. They only saw the abundance, not in how it came to be by bread blessed, broken, and given by the one who in his blessing would one day be broken, his life given for them. This was not an easy crowd. All they could think of was how their ancestors received manna, a form of bread while in the wilderness. Bread from heaven they wanted.

Jesus tries again to clarify. "The true bread of God is the one who comes down from heaven and gives life to the world" (v. 33). They then demanded that Jesus give them that bread every day of their lives. Talk about people who follow their gut.

Jesus further clarifies. "I am the bread of life. Whoever comes to me will never be hungry again. . . . I have come down from heaven to do the will of God who sent me . . . . All who see his Son and believe in him should have eternal life" (vv. 35, 39–40). He tried. But while it was one thing that the powerful and rich couldn't tolerate him, it was more distressing, more troubling that those he really wanted to reach didn't get him either. All they heard was what they wanted to hear or what they could twist into what they think they heard.

Hey, you know what? Don't blame them. After all, he's saying this right in his home territory, only a little way from infamous Nazareth. Everyone knows his parents, his dad Joseph, and mother. What's this deal that he came down from heaven?

"Stop complaining about what I said," Jesus remarks (v. 43).

Did Jesus just tell them to shut their mouths?

"I am the bread of life! . . . Anyone who eats this bread will live forever; and this bread, which I will offer so the world may live, is my flesh" (vv. 48, 51).

What is that supposed to mean?

It's a sign, people. Listen one more time. Make the connection. Bread feeds your lives. I am like bread in that I want you to have life, and this is eternal life. "Anyone who eats this bread will live forever; and this bread, which I will offer so the world may live, is my flesh."

How can this man give his flesh to eat?

He won't drop it. "Unless you eat the flesh of the Son of Man and drink his blood, you cannot have eternal life within you. But anyone who eats my flesh and drinks my blood has eternal life . . . . For my flesh is the true food, and my blood is the true drink. Anyone who eats my flesh and drinks my blood remains in me, and I in him. . . . I am the true bread that came down from heaven" (vv. 53–56, 58).

Whoa! This kind of talk will get you nowhere! Eat your flesh and drink your blood? Besides sounding like you flew right out of a cannibalistic vampire movie, this is the stuff conspiracy theories are made of! Dial it back. Make some sense. Give us a fighting chance at this at least.

Granted, Jesus's words are tough to hear. Obviously, the people and Jesus were speaking on different planes. All the people could see was what they wanted from him.

That's right. Just get me through the day with what I need and want. Eternal life? Too big of a stretch there, not on our radar. We've seen what you can do. Now be the God we want.

To be fair, and equally not surprising, even the disciples told Jesus that what he said was way over their heads and hard for anyone to accept. "Does this offend you?" he asked (v. 61). He knows what he's up against even within his own ranks. "The Spirit alone gives eternal life. Human effort accomplishes nothing. And the very words I have spoken to you are spirit and life" (v. 63). Accept what God has taken up for you, raised in blessing, broken apart, and given for you. Take it in, make it part of you, let God do what God does so you may be reversed and transformed into who God made you to be.

Probably choking then on his own words, Jesus admits, "But some of you do not believe me" (v. 64). With this, many followers deserted him (v. 66). They either weren't going to get what they wanted, or they didn't want what he had to give, or both. Turning, then, to his inner crew, the Twelve, he asks if they're leaving too. Peter stands for them and for him: "Lord, to whom would we go? You have the words that give eternal life. We believe, and we know you are the Holy One of God" (vv. 68–69). These words should have pushed back the building trouble around him. But Jesus knew fully what he was up against. "I chose the twelve of you, but one is a devil" (v. 70). The one who would bring all the trouble crashing down on him, Judas, remained among them (v. 71).

Who Is This Man?

As close as they were to Jesus, as much as his inner circle experienced more than just his work and message, the disciples seemed to have the roughest time getting what Jesus was about. To them, Jesus revealed more often the full extent of his power in who he was. Those crazy boat trips where people trailed Jesus on the Sea of Galilee were nothing compared to what these twelve followers experienced that night.

After such a huge miracle that touched not just the sick but fed all who came that day, Jesus had gone alone into the hills to rest and be restored. Expecting Jesus to return to their boat, the disciples waited until dark for him. When he didn't return, they must have figured he'd gone on foot back to Capernaum on the other side of the lake. Skilled fishermen as several of them were, they pushed off, even though it was already late. Soon an unexpected gale wind came up, and the sea waters rocked and pitched the boat, making their rowing futile. When doom seemed certain, they saw Jesus in the distance walking on the water, like a ghostly figure. Now real terror struck. They didn't know what they were seeing. Jesus called out, "Don't be afraid. I am here!" (v. 20). They pulled him in and found somehow their boat was safely at its destination (v. 21). But this wasn't their only adventure on the high seas.

Another time Jesus somehow was sleeping, conked out in the boat, like he's dead to the world, right in the middle of a "fierce storm" (Matthew 8:24). Translations belie the impact. The Greek word is *megas* as in a megastorm—a violent, exceedingly powerful outburst of nature, a no-way-you're-going-to-live-through-this kind of tumultuous storm. Waves filled the boat until it was nearly swamped. And yet, Jesus still slept through it like nothing was going on.

The disciples woke up Jesus, but not just to make him aware of what was going on. They level an accusation at him: "Don't you care . . . ?" (Mark 4:38). *Don't you care we are going down? Don't you care about us? Don't you care for your own life? What's with you, Jesus? Wake up to what's happening!*

May we just say there are times we can relate. When the pain, anxiety, or trauma is beyond what we can handle, it feels like God's not paying attention. Their question makes sense to us. Are we so expendable that you would sleep, not have a concern in all of creation as to what might happen to us? Are we that inconsequential to you in the big scheme of whatever life means? God, don't you care?

Or did the fact they called out to him have within it something else? Was there a belief that when all else is lost, God can step in? Stupidly funny, but there are those who think they have to handle everything on their own up until the last minute. What's more, the disciples still addressed him at a time like this as rabbi.

Did they expect Jesus had a little lesson in this yet still to share? Where were their minds? Were they wrapped up in a nice Sabbath sermon before a good lunch and an afternoon nap? These people need to take a walk on real streets for a change.

However, on the level of all good familiar plot lines, the conflict is resolved, the threat is removed, the storm is calmed.

Fine, for those who can sit with this. But for some, this kind of story is a deal breaker, the kind that raises bigger doubts that refuse to accept some kind of superhero sweeping in to tackle and eradicate the bad issues in our world. Doesn't happen very much, at least as far as most people can see.

Fair enough. Jesus spoke into the wind. He ordered it to calm down, to be quiet, to shut up. Strangely, though, he spoke as if to an intelligent creature calling for its silence, a reversal of its power and impact on the world. And it obeyed! He stilled the violent, life-threatening storm.

In the immediate resulting calm, Jesus asked his friends why they were afraid. He returned the accusation they brought upon him by his own question, "Do you still have no faith?" (v. 40).

The Twelve had no answer. That is, they couldn't even speak to give any kind of answer. They were struck with wonderment mixed with terror, amazement, and reverence. Their response was *megas*, the same as the size and force of the storm. All they had left was their own question, "Who is this man? . . . Even the winds and waves obey him!" (Matthew 8:27). They were given a revelation that this man, this Jesus as Son of God, was beyond their understanding. He had a cosmic power that spoke into the existential questions of life.

All questions don't get fully answered. Yet they are proposed to bring about, if not a stronger faith, at least the strength to live with a faith that can stand in the midst of questions. Does God care? The question only seems asked during a storm. When seas are calm, the sun shines, winds are a gentle, a cooling breeze waifs through, God's love is unquestioned. In the storms, though, when loved ones are deathly sick, when destitution is imminent, when relationships are on the rocks, when injustice is rampant and war rages, God takes those questions, those calls for succor, and hears within them the same force of a howling, raging sea.

Fear is inherent to life. It can be a healthy fear, steering one away from the destructive. But to remain in an anxiety which shouts that all is lost is what tears apart and drowns out any meaning to life. This is not a lesson in a therapeutic wish that faith will always bring about a desired outcome. Faith is not a promise that will always calm the storm, but it does ride into it.

"Who is this man?" the disciples ask among themselves. Time after time, Jesus gave the people, and more so the disciples, the answer to who he was—the one with power over nature, disease, and more, one sent from

God to reveal himself as Son of God. Yet even for those individuals closest to him, he was sometimes too much to take in, bringing trouble to him from inside his own ranks.

The Unexpected One

Out of compassion, Jesus gave people what they needed, but often his miracles pitched him between an individual's pain and social criticism that would deny attributing to him genuine divine power. Such it was when Jesus saw a beggar who had been blind since birth. As his disciples observed the man, they asked for the origin of his blindness. In this century, any kind of unexplained and untreatable disease was assumed to be caused by sin, and they concluded his affliction was a judgment upon the sin of the blind man or of his parents. Yet Jesus gave them another perspective. He told them that this man was born blind "so the power of God could be seen in him" (John 9:3). Jesus then cryptically made a statement about not much time being left for the assigned tasks to be done because night was coming (v. 4). "But while I am here in the world, I am the light of the world" (v. 5).

Then, spitting in the dust, Jesus made a paste of mud, smoothed it on the man's eyes, and told him to go wash. "So the man went and washed and came back seeing!" (v. 7). The Light of the World had pushed away the darkness of this man's life. That should have been cause for celebration, but only divisive trouble followed.

Some neighbors doubted that this now seeing man was the same one who had been begging on the roadside; others said it was he (v. 8). Pharisees, claiming Jesus was a sinner, interrogated the man. One faction said that the fact that Jesus healed on a Sabbath day proved he was a sinner; others asked how one in sin could do such miracles. Some doubted the formerly blind man really had been born blind (vv. 16, 18). They called in the man's parents, but fearing the religious leaders, they denied knowing how their son could now see (vv. 20–21).

A second interrogation of the man occurred. The leaders insisted that Jesus was a sinner. All the cured man could say to them was that he didn't know if Jesus was a sinner. "But I know this," he replied, "I was blind, and now I can see!" (v. 25). From there, the situation went from bad to worse. Pressed again for how he was healed, the man in frustration repeated what he had already told his religious interrogators. Questioning their motives, he asked, "Do you want to become his disciples, too?" (v. 27). For that, he was cursed. They claimed that they follow only Moses while Jesus was an unknown entity to them (vv. 28–29).

Sometimes it's not a good idea to preach to preachers. Backed into a corner, the man declared, "God doesn't listen to sinners, but he is ready to hear those who worship him and do his will. . . . If this man were not from God, he couldn't have done it" (vv. 31, 33). The insult was too much. "Are you trying to teach us?" the religious leaders snapped (v. 34). Cursed again as a sinner, they expel the healed man from participation in the synagogue. Whatever hope he had to finally become a vital part of the community was smashed. He may have to start begging again.

Later, Jesus found him. It was an interesting meeting because although he could now see, the man had never seen his healer. When Jesus had told him to go and wash, he went blindly in more ways than one, following his directions, not having any vision yet to see Jesus. In their conversation, Jesus first revealed his identity as the Son of Man (vv. 35–37). Both declaring his belief and now fully sighted, the healed man worshipped Jesus. Then Jesus gave him more, the purpose of the miracle: "to give sight to the blind and to show those who think they see that they are blind" (v. 39).

To change a person's perspective, mind, and heart can be as great an effort as to change their physical conditions. Release from spiritual blindness as well as the physical are both miracles. It happened for one man, and it happened for many to see and believe that Jesus's coming meant he brought life in all its fullness. The miracle was not just that Jesus could heal. It was also a sign that pointed to him as the Son of God. Still, this miracle also brought accusations by Jesus of blindness and guilt upon the Pharisees. That could only mean trouble.

> Excuse me, Jesus, but there's a question that's been hanging over all of this. Healings and other reversals of the natural world are great—great for the obvious reasons in relieving suffering, and if you need it, great that they reveal who you are as Son of God. But is that it? Do we have to suffer to make you look good so you can look like God? Is that how you love us? Do we have to suffer so we have to be dependent on you? Sure, like the blind man and the equally poor-sighted Pharisees, humanity can be myopic. Yet can't you raise the curtain on who you are without putting us through all of the pain and heartache?

Valid question. Life is rough. When the worst is thrown at us, we think it'd be helpful to know why. As it is, though, the why question is futile. Is there ever any good reason for suffering? When you sit in anguish, will any purpose for it be enough? Does even sacrifice for another make it good and right when the loss is beyond relief, when daily pain only inflicts all the more? People come up with all kinds of things to say. "It must be God's will." Or "We grow stronger in our trials." Or "Someday we'll understand." Fill in your own cliché. Does it ever work? Does it ever make the suffering better?

Jesus knew that the better answer to suffering doesn't concern the why but the who. Who will be there with us? Who will come alongside us to see us through? Who will love us no matter what? It's him, that's who. He is the greatest source of compassion. Jesus was there for those who sought him out and begged for his help and healing. "He healed every kind of disease and illness. . . . Whatever their sickness or disease, or if they were demon possessed or epileptic or paralyzed—he healed them all" (Matthew 4:23–24). Despite their limited understanding of who he was and his mission, the Son of God still reached out to relieve and restore.

In the end, it's obvious healings and cures are only temporary, only buying time until the inevitable end—the grave. Jesus knew this because he would enter and go through his own kind of suffering in order to reverse the outcome of that inevitability. That would be his final sign.

Maybe what hurt Jesus most, what was most troubling, was while his healing power convinced some people that he was the Son of God, his power also created, even in his best of friends, expectations which demonstrated how selfish people can be even in their relationship with God. Mary, Martha, and Lazarus were good friends with Jesus. Mary had sat at his feet when he taught and had anointed him with perfume to show her devotion. When Lazarus fell ill, Mary and Martha sent for Jesus. Why not? They knew of his work, they believed in his power, so they could call upon him to do what they needed. But for reasons not understood even to the disciples, Jesus waited two days. "Lazarus's sickness will not end in death. No, it happened for the glory of God so that the Son of God will receive glory from this" (John 11:4). Jesus told his disciples that Lazarus's death would give them another opportunity to "really believe" in him (v. 15). It will be another sign, and again it will bring trouble.

Upon Jesus's arrival, Lazarus had already been dead four days, and both Martha and Mary separately met Jesus with identical words: "Lord, if only you had been here, my brother would not have died" (vv. 21, 32). The overtones in their words raised the question, are they blaming him? Are they saying, you are the Son of God, and you are not supposed to treat us like this? Martha even added, "I know that God will give you whatever you ask" (v. 22). Is this a statement of faith or manipulation? She went on to say all the right things and declared that Jesus is the Son of God, but somehow she missed the point when he said to her, "I am the resurrection and the life" (v. 25). "Thy will be done" is not implied when she said, "Lord, if only you had been here." Her words sounded more like, "Lord, this is the problem, and this is what you need to do." It seems that the sisters' belief caused them to think that they could best serve God in an advisory capacity.

Apparently, Martha was the one who knew how to get things done. She ran to get her sister Mary and said that Jesus wanted to see her. Interestingly, that is not actually stated in the text. Maybe it can be assumed that Jesus did ask for Mary. But Lazarus's death was a big event, and there were people close to Jesus, listening to his every word. Did Martha put words in Christ's mouth? Was she trying to call in some support and triangulate with the sister who sat at his feet listening to him teach?

Mary told Jesus what Martha already had: "Lord, if only you had been here, my brother would not have died" (v. 32). Upon seeing her weeping and the other mourners, "Jesus wept" (v. 35). Known as the shortest verse in the Bible, these two words portray how upset Jesus had become. Often this is read as he was overcome with grief. However, a more accurate translation of the original Greek would be that he was very angry and indignant. Out of his anger and his frustration, Jesus wept.

Now here's the hard part. Two sisters are in grief over their brother's death. Mary, Martha, and Lazarus were close to Jesus. It is a nice picture of Jesus crying over his friend's grave. Why? Because it makes Jesus like the rest of humanity. If he cries over a good friend dying, then he'll sympathize with human grief.

> It kind of makes God like us, doesn't it? When he raises Lazarus, it's so we don't have to cry.

But here's the point, and why Jesus was so upset. The sisters and the crowd all had the same thought: if he could heal a blind man, then why didn't he keep Lazarus from dying in the first place?

Well, why didn't he? If we know Jesus can heal, and if he really loved all of them, then he should have. God can do these kinds of things. Why doesn't he?

Once again, the story ends well. Lazarus's mourners got what they wanted. Jesus called Lazarus out of the grave. Call it new birth or new life, and all is good (vv. 41–44).

Or is it? To understand this miracle is to understand what was being asked of Jesus and to understand why he raised Lazarus from the dead. Why Jesus was so upset was that people want miracles to solve their problems and make them feel good, to keep them out of pain. So he was being asked to fix the problem of Lazarus's death. *God, my brother is dead. You could have stopped it four days ago; you didn't. Now make a miracle; get your Father in heaven to change this. Lord, if you only had been here . . .*

We hear them. God, you know that all this evil and pain is not what you want and neither do we, so get rid of it. Then we'll know your kingdom of heaven.

Jesus wept. What frustrated and angered him so much was this pressure from those who should have understood best that his miracles were not meant only to fix a problem in someone's life but to give unmistakable proof that he was the Son of God. The accusations, blame, and manipulation showed him that this wasn't happening. The message wasn't getting through.

"Because of the miraculous signs Jesus did . . . , many began to trust him. But Jesus didn't trust them, because he knew all about people" (2:23–24). He knew they believed because they thought they had the Messiah they wanted, The Divine Fixer.

No one needed to tell him about human nature.

The one who had caused so much trouble was in deeper trouble now.

Jesus wept.

Further Provocations for Your Consideration

1. Jesus's "messianic assertions would have been completely discounted if not for the signs revealed in his miracles—great reversals of the natural processes of illness, disease, and even death." This chapter is premised on Jesus performing acts that were beyond the usual processes of the natural order. The intended effect was to give proof that he was the Son of God. If he had not performed miracles, how might that have impacted his followers? How have these miracle narratives impacted the understanding of Jesus in the present time?

_____

_____

_____

_____

_____

2. The question of suffering has been posed and wrestled over for eons. What various reasons for it are posited? Does God cause suffering, or is suffering where God meets the created world? What significance is there in that Jesus experienced suffering?

_____

_____

_____

_____

_____

3. Is suffering a punishment or judgment, as the disciples thought about the beggar who they believed was blind due to his or his parents' sin? What examples from today show that this is still an underlying, if not overtly stated, belief?

_____

_____

_____

_____

_____

4. Does God heal today? Are cures and healing brought about by great minds who develop treatments and remedies, or does God have a part in those developments?

_____

_____

_____

_____

_____

5. Do miracles that are a direct intervention of God happen today? Explain.

_____

_____

_____

6. When suffering, pain, and loss are not relieved, when the inevitable end comes to pass, where is God? Explain how death can be a form of healing.

_____

_____

_____

_____

_____

_____

7. The philosophy of randomness in the universe gives no rhyme or reason to the good or evil, blessing or hurt, that anyone can experience. In light of Jesus entering as God in the world, how is this perspective adjusted?

_____

_____

_____

_____

_____

_____

8. "Disease can be a great leveler." Explain how this is so.

_____

_____

_____

7

He Got Killed

Jesus wept.

Those who saw him didn't get it; maybe they never would. The troublemaker who had sought to change the world for them could not make them change. Jesus kept encountering people who were no different from those who oppressed them, no different from the serpent that ensnared them. "You won't die!" the snake had told the woman in the garden (Genesis 3:4). But what she heard was: *You can reverse what God has done. You will live forever. You won't have disease; you can have whatever or whomever you want when you want it.* Voices throughout the centuries have expanded the options: *Immediate gratification is yours because you have a Savior you can manipulate into your heavenly Daddy who grants your every wish; sure, loving neighbor and sharing wealth are great as long as I get what I want out of it.*

And the Son of God cries.

Likely not a day had passed before the high council of the Sanhedrin met. They knew the threat Jesus made in bringing Lazarus back from the dead, and they knew how to frame the issue so the evil they plotted looked necessary. "If we allow him to go on like this, soon everyone will believe him. Then the Roman army will come and destroy both our Temple and our nation" (John 11:48). This Jesus would cause the ultimate trouble because those in control would lose their control.

In reality, the religious leadership were only pawns of the Romans, tolerated as long as they kept the people corralled so they wouldn't revolt against the regime. Small-time marshals they were, nothing else. Even so, what little authority and power they had was a lot to lose for them. Jesus simply would not compromise, deal with them, or be complicit with the system. Enough was enough. Caiaphas, their high priest, spoke the most truthful statement of his clerical life. And like most truths, the full meaning of his statement would not be realized for generations. "It's better for you that one man should die for the people than for the whole nation to be destroyed" (v. 50). Thus, he would die for the people, that is, for "all the children of God scattered around the world" (v. 52). Jesus would die, and the trouble would be fulfilled.

He cried, but he'd known it all along. He tried to tell the Twelve, but usually they wouldn't hear it. They followed him, yes, but not for the right reasons. Jesus had asked them outright, "Who do you say I am?" (Matthew 16:15). They had the right answer, at least to a point. "You are the Messiah" (v. 16). You are the Promised One, the one who will deliver God's chosen people and restore the nation to the strength and glory it had under their ancestral king, David. Yes, call him Messiah. God had promised a Savior.

But this inner circle needed to adjust their expectations. Jesus would reign, but his victory would come not by an uprising against power but in a laying down, relinquishing his life to those who would have him destroyed and forgotten. He said suffering would be his weapon, sacrificial death would be his fate, and victory would be achieved in a reversal of death by the third day. Peter considered this kind of talk misguided. In private, he tried to counsel his Lord. The frustration and fight rose again, sitting just below the surface as when he had cleared the temple with a whip or broken down in tears. Jesus knew the source of Peter's words and where his train of thought was going.

"Get away from me, Satan!" (v. 23). Jesus's words spit back into those forty days in the desert. In spite of his weakened state, there he had wrestled with his destiny, slammed and punched back the devil. Hungry, alone in the wilderness for way too long, it took all he had. Jesus survived that round but not altogether whole, for following his struggle, angels came and cared for him. He likely had wept then as well. They would meet again (Mark 1:12–13).

> Dear, dear Jesus, oh Son of Man, you gotta just calm down. Really, calling your best man a "Satan"? Peter was just trying to talk some sense into you. He'd already settled it. You are the Messiah. The twelve in your crew are behind you. Now organize your heavenly forces, march into Jerusalem, and take that city. All of Israel will flock to your side, and the filthy Romans will flee fast on the roads they built for themselves. Face it. You are the man! Later you can carry on your mission to change souls.

If only . . . but that wasn't the plan. "You are seeing things merely from a human point of view, not from God's," Jesus said (Matthew 16:23).

> You mean God wanted the chosen ones of Israel to live under Roman rule forever? What's wrong with wanting to better your life, have an ambition to achieve more, turn your hard work into a huge payday, sit back and enjoy the fruits of your labor? Isn't that what the world says, have it your way? What's God got against any of that?

It's not what God is against; it's what God is for. At this point, Jesus was trying to give his followers a clear-eyed picture of where they were heading.

Jerusalem was not going to be a fun festival. When they reached the city, they would be met not only with adoring crowds (most looking for a miracle show) but also with a mean collision with the religious and political leaders. Tensions would reach a tipping point. His adversaries would have to utilize their biggest weapon—the power to kill. Executions kept things quiet for a good while. Jesus would be in their crosshairs.

Still, he refused to play his enemies' game. Jesus said to his disciples and declared to the crowd that, to follow him, they must put aside their selfish desires, dreams, and purposes. Instead, they needed to lift and accept the cross given to them and get behind what he was doing and in the way he was doing it. "If you try to hang on to your life, you will lose it," he told them (Mark 8:35). Conversely, lose your life for God's sake, and you'll save it. It's a paradox that grapples with finding meaning in a life lived by relinquishing it for a larger, greater meaning.

Jesus said so much that his disciples didn't understand—all his parables of big banquets and seeds and fig trees. People followed him, but they didn't get what he was driving at, and the priests didn't get it even when it came out of their own mouths. But he knew. Jesus kept at it, repeatedly telling all who would listen how it would be.

The Sightless and Shepherds

He was being tracked and stalked. Already, he nearly got stoned in the temple (John 8:59). Then, Jesus had another one of his tussles with the Jewish leaders. Of course, it was over some good thing he did. He had healed that blind man, both physically and spiritually, for this guy could not only see but he saw Jesus as Messiah. Not so for the infuriated Pharisees. They had been looking for dirt on Jesus but couldn't find any, so they had to twist the truth. They turned his healing on the Sabbath day into a violation of Sabbath law. You know, the Sabbath when you're not supposed to work? Oh, put aside this was a miracle, unexplainable, not according to natural order occurrence. Thou shall not do miracles on the Sabbath day! Like everyone else was going around doing it (John 9).

In this tension, Jesus told a story of a good shepherd. On the surface, it's a sweet tale, very appropriate for children. Fuzzy white sheep translate well into cotton-balled crafts, and little ones love to know there's someone who'll defend them against the bad guys. Having a good shepherd helps with feelings of insecurity. Adults can relate, if only life could be that simple. If nothing else, though, Jesus never meant to give simple stories for simple answers. His subtlety goes deep.

In telling this story, he makes claims about himself. "I am the good shepherd." He describes devotion, love, care, and concern, an intimate relationship between the good shepherd and his sheep. They belong to the shepherd, and he will do what it takes, even give his own life willingly, for them to know his devotion. Contrast the good shepherd with the hired hand. Any hint of danger, like a wolf coming to attack, kill, and destroy, and that hired guy takes off running. The sheep aren't his, and he couldn't care less what happens to them.

Now, in this story, if Jesus is the good shepherd, who do you think the hired hand might be? The ones who didn't care that a man who'd been born blind was just healed except that it happened on the wrong day of the week? Not far under its surface, this isn't a nursery, bedtime story, safe and cute for innocent children.

Characteristically, Jesus doesn't leave it at that. Again, he says, "I am the good shepherd." He compares how close he is with his sheep with a closeness he has with his Father. And what does a good shepherd do? He lays down his life for his sheep.

Jesus made some radical claims here. First, he loved people more than the Jewish leaders did because they thought of themselves before the welfare of others. Hold on to the Sabbath because if that law goes, the whole Ten Commandments might collapse. Where would their control over the people be then?

Then he had said that he was close to his Father, like Jesus and God were of one mind or spirit. That really went over an edge.

> This guy sounds dangerous.

Jesus added to it. He says there are "other sheep," not yet in the sheepfold. They also hear his voice as shepherd, not only hear it, but listen to his voice. Eventually, they will be included so there will be just one flock.

> Who are these other sheep? Outsiders, strangers, wanderers, foreigners, people who don't look like us? This guy is a fanatic.

By this point, the Jewish leaders likely had hands over their ears and were wailing to drown out how Jesus concluded this story. He spoke of the love his Father had for him, and now repeated three more times that he would give up, lay down, willingly surrender his life for his sheep. To know that God desires to gather everyone, inclusive of all souls, in love is a lesson from one who loves the world so much that nothing would stop what was necessary to save them.

Bravely, pointedly, right into the faces of trouble, Jesus faced down those who would just as soon see him dead, telling this story of a God who loves without discrimination. He could have told a story of celestial battles or God calling down judgment or something big and bold and designed to get people to straighten up. But no, he told a story about sheep who follow their good shepherd because he loves them so much. As it was, both his closest friends and worst enemies didn't get it. That kind of trouble will make you cry (10:11–21).

It had been three years since Jesus's ministry began. While the miracles had set him apart and revealed just a small part of his divinity, the lessons and stories explained his identity and promise of a life that fulfilled one's created purpose.

Living Water

The Samaritan woman at the well wanted what all the rest had wanted. The Good Shepherd was working outside the sheepfold when he asked her for a drink. Surprised that he even asked, she calls him out about it: Jews don't talk with Samaritans; women don't talk with strange men. That said, Jesus sidesteps her comments. He tells her, "I would give you living water," water that takes away thirst altogether. To those who drink it, "it becomes a fresh, bubbling spring within them, giving them eternal life" (John 4:10, 14). That was enough. Like that first woman in the garden, she only heard what she wanted to hear. "Give me this water! Then I'll never be thirsty again, and I won't have to come here to get water" (v. 15). *Yeah, come on God, make my life easy. Take away the toil of life. Don't leave me here slaving away, just trying to survive.* What was that last thing he said, eternal life? The chorus has heard that before: "You won't die!" She didn't get it, just like the others.

"Go and get your husband," he says to her (v. 16).

Quickly she responds, "I don't have a husband" (v. 17).

Then Jesus commends her: "You're right! You don't have a husband—for you have had five husbands, and you aren't even married to the man you're living with now" (v. 17). Dangerous territory Jesus tread, revealing who she really is—a woman who never made a relationship work and couldn't get the man she's with now to marry her.

Five husbands she's had? A Samaritan outside the Jewish law but not outside Jesus's understanding of her. Used, passed around like a commodity, in reality she wasn't married but rather owned by men, and the man in her life now wouldn't give her at least the outward sign of propriety. The village gossips gathered at the well, and so she had to come in the heat of the day to draw water, avoiding the shame of those who knew her real life. And now there was no escaping it from the man with whom she was conversing.

Starved for real relationship, she continues, deflecting into talk about where is the proper place to worship. Jesus comes back with the very element she avoids: "For God is spirit, so those who worship him must worship in spirit and in truth" (v. 24). Truth: the very thing lacking in her life, the very thing she ran away from and yet could not escape, the truth which she sought but could not understand. She needed a Messiah to explain everything. "I AM the Messiah!" he tells her (v. 26).

She runs to the village and brings people back to hear and see the one who offers living water. So it was, an outsider, a woman, was among the first to bring people to Jesus.

Jesus's disciples return, knowing he hasn't eaten, but he refuses to partake. "My nourishment comes from doing the will of God, who sent me, and from finishing his work" (v. 34). He could only be fed, energized in body and soul, when the people listened and believed. At least on that day, one life changed by a short conversation became the life that spread the message of new life to countless others (vv. 28–30, 39–42).

New Wine and Sacrifice

Yet, coupled with his message must be that which is more. If not accepted as proof, it is a sign of his identity. His first miracle revealed what his divinity also would do through his humanity, his coming trouble. Jesus faced it and looked deep into it that day when his mother approached him in the middle of a wedding feast and said to him, "They have no more wine" (John 2:3). Jesus answered, "Dear woman, that's not our problem" (v. 4). It wasn't his responsibility to do anything about this need. After all, he, his mother, and his disciples were guests, not hosts.

Of course, Jesus knew what was yet to come: the clamoring for healing, for food, even for the water that would take away thirst and the need to draw from deep wells every day. But there was more to his mission than asking God to take away the burdens of life, that which detracts from feeling in control and in charge of life. So he told his mother, "My time has not yet come" (v. 4).

His mother said nothing to him but turned to the servants. Years before she had told the angel who revealed to her that she would soon bear God's Son, "I am the Lord's servant. May everything you have said about me come true" (Luke 1:38). Now that she had birthed and reared him, she did what her ancestors had done, what God ultimately asks of parents, and handed her firstborn son back to God. Hebrew people knew the pattern: Abraham had lifted a knife over Isaac, Moses' mother had placed him in a basket on the Nile River, Hannah had taken Samuel to the high priest Eli, and Mary likewise would do the same. "Do whatever he tells you," she told the servants (John 2:5). To her son, though, her direction meant, accept the trouble you now are going to start, and the trouble you will know. Would these words haunt her three years later? Yet, also with these words, Mary fulfilled the divine task given to her as the Lord's servant; she handed him back to God; her service was complete.

Six stone waterpots were standing there. (No, it wasn't time!) They held twenty to thirty gallons each. (But it wasn't the right time!) They were supposed to be set aside, not for common use but for ceremonial purposes of washing just as the law stipulated. This was a wedding that belonged to a couple. (This just wasn't the right time!) Water from these pots was to cleanse the body and speak to the soul. There would be time for that water later.

As Jesus gazed at the pots, did he see his time to come? Time at Jacob's well, time when the stormy seas would rage, time when he would pour water into a basin for washing feet, time when he would gasp those words, "I thirst." Yet Jesus knew, as his mother charged him, his time for trouble to begin had come.

As he directed, the servants filled the pots with ordinary water and then poured some which they took to the wedding master of ceremonies. The host was surprised! His servants brought him excellent wine, much better than that which was first served to the guests. Jesus knew what the water had become. While viewed as a miracle to the servants and the disciples, he knew the more that had occurred. And his disciples believed in him, their Messiah. Later, however, he declared himself as one who does not right their world in all that is wrong. Instead, he would give them living water to quench their deepest spiritual needs and make them into more than what they were created to be.

So ordinary water poured into cups became wine. And as the one who brings living water, his very life will be poured as into a cup. His time had not yet come, but that time would come.

Gathered around a low table with the Twelve, there would be wine again poured into a cup, and he would explain what it meant. He would tell his closest followers as he offered the cup, "Take this and share it among yourselves. . . . This cup is the new covenant between God and his people—an agreement confirmed with my blood, which is poured out as a sacrifice for you" (Luke 22:17, 20). Living water had become wine, and now wine becomes blood. The trouble is that the blood would be his. It would not be the first blood to ever have been spilled. From the animal that died to clothe the man and woman in the garden, to the first brother who would die by his own brother's hand, to the wars that have destroyed and the fights that have ended in slaughter, to executions of the criminal alongside the innocent, blood has been shed for all kinds of reasons—from grasps for power and wealth to the defense of peace. But no blood-shedding in history would be like his blood. His blood had to challenge the trouble of the world, the call of all who have hoped to know, "You won't die." Only his blood could reverse that which would separate all who have breathed from the God who gives breath. "You won't die" could not be obtained by grabbing perceived power but only by accepting the one who is the source of the greatest power known, the power of Love. The Good Shepherd, our hero, had to face his demise, and it was by his virtue that he would know his biggest trouble—his very death.

Welcome the King!

His time finally came.

Jesus entered Jerusalem to the cries of children and a fired-up crowd. Everyone came out to see the spectacle of Jesus riding into Jerusalem on a young donkey. All accounts record it. It must have been quite the procession. People spread their coats on the ground, and the road was strewn with leafy branches to make the ride smoother and keep down the dust. Clamorous voices called him a king, the one who would establish a new kingdom on the level of their greatest hero, King David. The chorus shouted, "Blessing on the one who comes in the name of the Lord!" (Mark 11:9), fulfilling what the ancient prophets had promised. Not lost on anyone was the celebration of Passover only days away, the commemoration of the Israelite deliverance from slavery and oppression by the Egyptians. Part parade, part protest, however you see it, God was on the move and doing it again!

The story that Jesus actually had raised a man from the dead had gone viral. Lazarus, who had been dead, and not just for a few minutes and revived, but four days dead. His relatives even had to open up the man's tomb, and in a loud voice Jesus had shouted for him to come out. And the guy did, grave clothes and all! With that, the Jews believed now was their time. Life was going to change in a big way. If Jesus could raise the dead, those Roman oppressors might as well pack up and run for the hills. Hope was so big you could taste it.

When the parade was over, when the shouting had quieted, when the crowds were finally gone, Jesus went into the temple in Jerusalem and looked around carefully at everything. After the day he just had, maybe he cried again. The most significant week of his life was before him. People wanted so much from him, but what they wanted was not for him to give.

Trouble was they watched him, heard his words, and put their hopes in him, seeing only what they wanted to see and wanted to hear, not what God was offering them for their souls.

"Hosanna," they had shouted (v. 9 NIV). Their cry was not as it seems, what they wanted it to be, even what we have been told it is. Hosanna is not so much a praise but a plea. What the crowd called out for but did not understand in truth was "Save us!"

He would. He would be their king, more so of their hearts than their country. He would bring about a new kingdom. In fact, by him it was already beginning, the kingdom of God. Raising someone from the dead was only a sign of the new reality he would establish. He would make that reality full, answering their plea to save by turning it into their salvation (Mark 11:1–11; John 12:12–18).

None of this was lost on those who had the most to lose. Maybe if they had not been so paranoid over maintaining their status and its benefits, they would have relaxed a little. But that procession got them into nearly as big a frenzy as the crowd. "This is getting us nowhere. Look how the whole world has gone after him!" the Pharisees lamented (John 12:19). Actually, in some ways Jesus did their work for them.

Among those people going to worship at the feast in Jerusalem were some out-of-towners, Greeks who may have been trained in logic and philosophy. Likely, they had come to observe for themselves this religious high point of the year for Jews. Yet, there was this new guy who people were saying had a different take on the law. Some people thought he might be the Messiah that the ancient prophets had promised would deliver the Jews from Roman control. Why not hear his take on life's meaning? This was right up their alley. "We want to meet Jesus," they said (v. 21). Sounds simple enough. Listen to him teach, maybe have a good philosophical dialogue, shake hands, and on with the rest of their itinerary.

Jesus had plenty to say, but it wasn't a dialogue, a give-and-take time of questioning, proposing alternatives. There was no small talk, welcoming as equals, light discussion of the events of the day. Jesus didn't assume a role; he is what he is. He told it outright. "The time has come," he began (v. 23). Not exactly an overt statement, but a nod to the trouble to come. He put them on notice to be expectant, for God was going to move—the Son of Man was going to get his glory. Unexpectedly, characteristically, he took this differently from illustrations of adoration, triumph, celestial celebration. He related it to how a kernel of wheat had to die before it could grow and produce a bountiful harvest of wheat. You've got to listen hard to catch up with him sometimes. Then he said, "Those who love their life in this world will lose it. Those who hate their life in this world will keep it for eternity" (v. 25).

> Speaking for those Greek visitors and the rest of us listening in, what in the heavens and on earth can you possibly mean? Love and life are not meant to be thrown away. They're precious, so you protect that which you love, especially life. But you're saying to hate our precious lives so we can keep them? Pastor of the paradox, you certainly are!

Certainly love is precious and drives much of life. Yet, where you place that love, that loyalty, your life's dedication—that is his point. If you want to meet Jesus, you must meet him where he is. "Come, and follow me," he said. To do so is to refute much of what you think you must have to live, to survive, to be happy in this world. One's right to oneself is sacrificed to being his follower, his disciple.

> This is too much, really. So all I've worked for, everything I've become, is completely out the window? Dear God, but how can you ever ask this of us?

Granted, it's a lot. A whole lot. Wimps need not apply. Jesus asked for rethinking what's central, what right now may seem non-negotiable, the I-can't-ever-live-without things of life. If not an immediate one-eighty reversal, it would require a lifetime of peeling of the onion in finding what is the pristine core of what makes life worth living. Maybe that's the purpose of the exercise. In all, though, Jesus wants to be that central thing. But don't think that's too much to ask of someone. He knows.

Jesus knows because it was no less than what was asked of him. He struggled with it more than we'll ever know. "Should I pray, 'Father, save me from this hour?'" he asked of himself as much as those around him. In anguished resolve, he prayed, "But this is the very reason why I came! Father, bring glory to your name" (v. 27). Before the week was out, he met his purpose of trouble, to be like that kernel of wheat and die, buried in the ground. The ultimate sacrifice we call it. Surely, God would not ask that of us, we hope.

Yet that kernel has to die as a seed before it can grow and produce a harvest. From a life sacrificed in following Jesus there reaps a life that will not die—a life that will last into eternity. Loss becomes gain, death reverses into life, letting go leads to finding more.

Over and over, he tried to advance his cause, especially during that last week. But his efforts seemed misdirected. Throwing the money changers and merchants out of the temple didn't help his cause. A parable about evil farmers who kill the vineyard owner's son was clearly aimed at the religious leaders. Then there was that diatribe right there in the temple in front of listening crowds directed at the sham of the religious teachers. Jesus warned, "Practice and obey whatever they tell you, but don't follow their example. For they don't practice what they teach" (Matthew 23:3). From there it got real ugly.

He mocked how they wore little boxes on their arms with ancient scripture inside, the way they loved to get the best seat at the banquet tables, the attention they got from everyone on the street. "Those who exalt themselves will be humbled, and those who humble themselves will be exalted" (v. 12). He shouted: "Hypocrites! For you are careful to tithe even the tiniest income from your herb gardens, but you ignore the more important aspects of the law—justice, mercy, and faith" (v. 23). Jesus called them out as so concerned about their outward appearances, while inside they were filthy, greedy, and self-indulgent, like whitewashed tombs holding decay, complicit even in their position as murderers of prophets. Snakes! Blind guides! Sons of vipers! Hypocrites! "What sorrow awaits you" (vv. 13, 15, 16, 23, 25, 27, 29). His polemic was troubling and threatening, crossing a major line as he challenged the religious elite. Afterward, Jesus left the temple grieving, regretful over its fate and that of Jerusalem (vv. 37–38).

Two days left. Two days until Passover. Good Jews prepared for this day of remembrance, this day of deliverance, this day which had begun their solidification as a people, as a nation. They gathered there in the Holy City, the site of the temple and the seat of God's presence. Jesus continued his teaching, his now almost desperate effort to explain and prepare his disciples for what was to come. He spoke of final days, bridesmaids needing oil for their lamps in anticipation of the bridegroom's arrival, of a shepherd who separates sheep and goats according to their service to those in need, those who in effect serve the King of kings. Jesus's time had almost come.

He connected that day with trouble. "As you know, Passover begins in two days" (Matthew 26:2). Good enough. All good Jews knew the elements of this special meal, the rituals that taught their story, their history, to the next generation. But while they were looking back, Jesus looked ahead: "the Son of Man, will be handed over to be crucified" (v. 2).

One disciple heard differently. Judas knew what he could do about it. The religious leaders had met at the home of Caiaphas to plot how to eliminate Jesus. For the price of thirty pieces of silver, Judas defected to their side and joined their conspiracy against Jesus. As a spy within the ranks, Judas would know Jesus's movements, when would be the best time to move on him (vv. 14–16).

It was finally time. Jesus gave the directive to his followers: "As you go into the city, you will see a certain man. Tell him, 'The Teacher says: My time has come, and I will eat the Passover meal with my disciples at your house'" (v. 18). This would be his last meal, his last Passover celebration. The end had begun. For this, he had come. He would meet his trouble, the trouble his mother had been told would pierce her very soul, the trouble he had tried to prepare his friends for, the necessary trouble.

> Jesus, let's think about this. Now is your time, but it doesn't have to be this way. You know what to do. Back off. Let those holy frauds calm down a bit. Reorganize your plan. Yes, you are the Son of God. But this? Suffering, laying down your life as you call it? Acting the part of the sacrificial lamb? Why a bloody death of all things? Just tell people you will wipe their slates clean if they get behind you. No, this isn't necessary. This doesn't have to be. Why, oh God, why do you do this! Who in their right mind would follow a leader who acts the loser?

Stop! You misunderstand. This time isn't about success, at least as you know it. How could you? This had never been done before. Your strategic plans have nothing like it. Besides, by this point in his story, what did you expect? Never was it said that Jesus ever bought into the go-along-to-get-along process of appeasement, a social greasing of the wheel. Jesus's way is contrary—contrary as a full reversal, opposite from expectations of achievement, and contrary in how obstinate, stubborn, resolute he was going to be to achieve it.

After breaking bread and lifting his cup with his closest friends, the hero no longer preaches, teaches, or heals. He accepts that which he has come to do. Later, in a garden, he begs, cries, wails to God that his blood-filled cup be taken away. "My Father!," Jesus calls out. "Let this cup of suffering be taken away from me" (v. 39). As a man, every cell of his being wants to run, flee, bolt, change this fate before him. He does not want to drink it. Anxiety and anguish flood his mind and body. "Yet," he adds with resolution, "I want your will to be done, not mine" (v. 39). Only because there is no other way for that promised hope, "You won't die," he drinks the cup of death and trouble.

The chorus mob of religious leaders and soldiers had their way, led by the traitor Judas. The conflict that had begun so long ago in an ancient garden built to its impending climax in another garden just outside of Jerusalem. Judas acted. Was it from greed, disappointed ambition, a power play to force Jesus to act out and establish Israel as a contender among nations? Or had Judas at least heard, hoped that this new kingdom could be different, the kingdom of God? Whatever the struggle, in an ironic display of identification, he approached Jesus and greeted him with a kiss (vv. 47–49).

In a propulsion of events, Jesus was led through a dizzying series of trials and judges. The religious high council distorted, perverted, and falsified his statements in order to charge him with crimes. Pilate, the Roman governor of Judea, tried to pass Jesus off on Herod Antipas, the tetrarch of Galilee and Perea, but Jesus wouldn't satisfy him with a miracle show. So Herod sent Jesus back to Pilate, and the two men, who had been enemies up to that point, became friends (Matthew 26:57–67; Luke 22:66–23:12).

Every year during Passover, a Jewish prisoner was released. Barabbas, a murderer and insurrectionist, was the first candidate, but Pilate, finding no real evidence against Jesus, offered the crowd an exchange. The mob, stirred up by the conspiracy story of the temple leaders, wouldn't accept it. Only Jesus's blood would satisfy them. Our chorus again screamed, but this time the words were filled with death: "Crucify him!" (Matthew 27:22). Pilate caved rather than risk a riot. Barabbas was released to them, and Jesus was turned over to Roman executioners. A whip slashed Jesus's back, a crown of thorns was pressed into his scalp, a beam from his cross was laid upon him, and he carried that to his execution site. There nails were driven into his wrists and feet. Later a sword was driven into his flesh. The one who so many had hoped would save the world was, for a while, owned by the trouble of the world (vv. 15–50; John 18:38–19:34).

Pilate, having futilely tried to wash his hands of his part in this rigged execution, attempted to further distance himself. He ordered that a plaque be displayed over Jesus as he hung on the cross: "This is Jesus, the King of the Jews" (Matthew 27:37).

See, can anything good come from Nazareth?

"You won't die" had separated the finest the Creator had made—his image bearers—from the rest of his creation. Trouble then followed, and its pain surfaced despite all the efforts to stop it. Death came. All would die.

Yet, therein lay the trouble with Jesus. He died at the hands of those who would hurt, harm, and control the world. In just a few hours, the Sabbath laws would take effect: thou shalt not labor let alone prepare a dead body for burial. Mutilated and crushed, our fallen hero was carried to a cave marked for the use of burial, and a heavy stone was placed at the entrance to seal his lifeless body. The Light of the world had been extinguished. Trouble was over, finally. For itself as much as for him, feeling weak and vulnerable the chorus sobbed. With him, it seemed, hope had died.

Further Provocations for Your Consideration

1. Sit with this. Jesus is dead. All the promises of abundant and eternal life die with him. God is dead. If anything, the one thing that helps cope with the troubles of life is hope. What now? Where is hope, where is promise, where do you go when cold death is the final trouble?

_____

_____

_____

_____

_____

_____

2. "If you try to hang on to your life, you will lose it." Conversely, lose your life for God's sake, and you'll find it. It's a paradox that grapples with finding meaning in a life lived by relinquishing it for a larger, greater meaning (Mark 8:31–38). What's the struggle in this? Where does the struggle originate? Leave aside the big names like Mother Teresa. Who are the average persons who do this kind of thing? It's been said that all behavior has benefit. What benefit is there in helping others under the banner of serving God? Do you fully believe that serving others brings significant meaning in life?

_____

_____

_____

_____

_____

_____

3. "It's not what God is against; it's what God is for." Explain how this statement impacts you.

_____

_____

_____

_____

_____

_____

_____

8

His Kind of Love

"Y ou won't die!" (Genesis 3:4). The serpent's lie is repeated, twisting through the ages, with the scorn and derision of an enemy who acts the victor.

The crowd mocked Jesus. They met his last words with ridicule and vengeance. "Father, forgive them, for they don't know what they are doing" (Luke 23:34).

> More like, forgive us for letting this kind of trouble trespass
> on us.

"He saved others," the crowd further mocked, so "let him save himself" (v. 35). And save us "while you are at it" (v. 39). Even one of the sinners hanging on a cross next to Jesus sneered at his suffering.

But not all witnesses to his execution spoke harshly to him. "Jesus, remember me when you come into your Kingdom," this other criminal said, sincerely, with faith. And Jesus answered him: "I assure you, today you will be with me in paradise" (vv. 39–43). How incredulous that must have sounded to Jesus's mockers. How can a dying and cursed man promise paradise to anyone? Jesus's words of promise about eternal life were absurd.

Most poignant was the presence of his mother among the few women who refused to desert her son, even as her dreams for him dissolved. She watched the horror, maybe hoping that it wouldn't consummate, that God would intervene. But she also knew that when Jesus was only eight days old at his temple dedication, the prophet Simeon had foretold, "A sword will pierce your very soul" (2:35). Simeon spoke those words directly to her. Now, standing before her hanging son, rocking between grief and shock, she felt those words now as much as the nails that were hammered into her son's hands and feet. Hadn't the angel said Jesus's kingdom would never end? Shouldn't that mean that Jesus would not die? The rejection she'd felt that time he had the audacity to say "Who is my mother?" was nothing compared to this cruel end (Matthew 12:48). Even now, he still called her woman. Her heart twisted as he didn't even acknowledge what she was to him, what she went through to have him, and how she gave him back to God that day at the wedding.

Knowing her torment, Jesus understood that her sacrifice was entwined with his. More than to comfort her, more than to honor her, out of his agony, Jesus spoke love to Mary, love of his mother and love of God for her acceptance of the trouble he brought. With the only disciple present at the cross, he said, "Dear woman, here is your son." And to John, he said, "Here is your mother" (John 19:26–27). John would care for Mary as his own, knowing that their shared intimate memories of Jesus would sustain the other. In this final provision, even as Jesus gasped his last words, he taught the sacredness and eternal connectedness of relationships.

Only a few women and one of his closest friends were witnesses from the many who had followed Jesus. All the crowds had gone, for he couldn't fix their problems from where he was now. His suffering was his alone to bear, as he again faced down his devil of an antagonist using the ancient Scriptures that had served him so well before. Jesus's agony called up a psalmist's words, "My God, my God, why have you abandoned me?" (Psalm 22:1; Mark 15:34). Brutally beaten, humiliated, and crucified, Jesus absorbed into himself the ugly, the hideous, the darkness, the worst of all humanity. The one who was God was as far away from God as trouble can separate.

The rest of his words came out of that despair. "I am thirsty" (John 19:28), he said. *I'm empty, I've given it all, my cup of living water, this blood-wine, is nearly drained and poured out.* "It is finished," he says (v. 30). *I'm here so they don't have to be, and I've taken all that the worst of them could devise. I've fulfilled my purpose.* "Father, I entrust my spirit into your hands" (Luke 23:46). *I can do no more. Thy will is done.*

Trouble is dead, but the one who changed water to wine, made the blind see and the lame walk, fed the hungry on next to nothing, and raised the dead is the one who would reverse what trouble brings. He would do the same for himself and all who live out of and from the very place that the most trouble lies—the cross and the grave.

Three days after his death and burial, appearing with real flesh and spirit, showing the scars of his execution in his hands and side, and later eating fish with his friends, he reversed the trouble. What was hoped for, he displayed for all. *You won't die because I did what you could not do. I met your trouble— the trouble you give and the trouble you get. I defeated death with that which the devil will never know and the world cannot fully give.* It took the greatest power in all of creation and beyond to do this. It took the very Love of God.

A Night to Remember

Three years earlier, Jesus had made a huge amount of trouble. It was a good night to go into hiding. The authorities were still steaming about his tirade with the money changers in the temple. When challenged by the temple leaders about his protest, he made a cryptic if not ridiculous claim: "Destroy this temple, and in three days I will raise it up" (John 2:19). Eventually his followers would understand its real meaning and import. But on that day, it only added to his trouble.

Later that night, requiring the cover of deep dark, after the crowds had been healed and the power brokers who made money off of them thought that Jesus's threatening influence had stopped, at least for a season, a figure slipped into the disciples' camp. By power and status, he was from the other side. No respectable Pharisee would be caught in the light of day with this troublemaker, but slipping through black shadows, Nicodemus approached Jesus.

He tried. Nicodemus began by calling Jesus teacher, rabbi. He affirmed that Jesus's miracles were signs, proof if you will, that God was with him. Or at least Nicodemus said so in order to get close, to flatter, even ingratiate himself with Jesus. But Jesus didn't fall for it. Immediately, pointedly, he declared to this Pharisee that to see or be a part of God's kingdom, you must be "born again" (3:3). Confused, perhaps feeling spiritually dense, Nicodemus asked if an old man could return into his mother's womb and be born again (v. 4). He had not expected Jesus to be irrational.

Let's get a better picture here. Nicodemus as a religious leader worked for those who wanted Jesus eliminated. He was risking a lot to even have a conversation with this radical rabbi. But he had seen, or at least heard about, some of the miracles attributed to Jesus. He went to Jesus seeking an honest inquiry. So why didn't Jesus talk with the poor guy on a level he could grasp? Makes you wonder if this is how Jesus comes at all of us.

To be fair, maybe it was just the way Jesus made his comment. Maybe if he had said that there needed to be changes in a person's life, changes in priorities that didn't require sacrificing self, it would have gone over better. Maybe if he had said that one could find God by keeping the commandments, attending the festivals, and making the sacrifices, Jesus would have been understandable. Maybe if he had used words that were already theologically accepted and understood or along philosophical lines of reaching into one's inner self to find one's best, his words would have been at least aspirational. But Jesus wasn't born into this trouble to just water it down to what people wanted to hear. Instead, he made more trouble. He wanted lives and their purpose completely reversed, so he used the imagery of being born again to convey his point.

Born again. As a baby is a clean slate for a life to be lived out, so the soul needs to be wiped cleaned, washed in water that is changed to blood, if you will, by life lived out in the Spirit of God. That Spirit is known by knowing one who came to show the extent of God's love. It is known by those who in their souls come to believe that Love will reverse forever their lives and destiny in this life and afterwards.

Finally, with just a handful of words, Jesus clarified this love: "God so loved the world . . ." (v. 16 NIV). That animal whose skin was given to cover the nakedness of the couple in the garden of Eden had to die. In that perfect place without any kind of trouble, a death had to happen so this man and woman would know the extent of their Creator's love. They had wanted to be more, to be like God, and they believed a lie to obtain it: Eat this and you will not die (Genesis 3:1–4). The trouble that this rebellion brought could only be defeated with a copious love that nothing in this world could stop or overwhelm.

"God so loved the world that he gave . . ." (John 3:16 NIV). His love took the fullest sacrifice that human beings could identify. His love spilled out and gave all it could. Costly? Yes, in all the trouble the world could bring. It meant a surrender that shatters all concept of a love that serves itself. As Jesus said of himself, "the Son of Man came not to be served but to serve others and to give his life as a ransom for many" (Mark 10:45). It's a self-sacrificial giving, a giving that is unselfish, that doesn't promote itself. It's love given that is total, unreserved, and unrestricted.

"God so loved the world that he gave his one and only Son . . ." (John 3:16 NIV). One can't know love without knowing the Lover. So the Lover, through his Son, came among those who live in trouble and are trouble. The Lover came to show what total love looks like and how love is done. "As the Father knows me," Jesus said, "I know the Father—and I lay down my life" (10:15 NIV). God knew what his love would cost, and there was no other way to deal with the trouble of the world except for him as the Son to face it directly.

"God so loved the world that he gave his one and only Son, that whoever believes in him . . ." (3:16 NIV). Jesus offered when he called individuals, "Come and see" (1:39). *Watch me, observe me, draw closer, get nearer to what I do and who I am. Know me for yourself and not just because of what you've been told or what someone else wants you to know.* "Come, follow me," he told them, "and I will show you how to fish for people" (Matthew 4:19). *And if you get close enough, I will change you and reverse all that you thought you were or could ever be. For in me you will know God and believe, in me you will have faith in what I can do, and in me you will trust as you walk in my path.*

"God so loved the world that he gave his one and only Son, that whoever believes in him will not perish . . ." (John 3:16 NIV). *Yes*, Jesus is saying, *that for which you've striven is what I want for you as well. You will not die! That inner sense of self you call your soul is greater than anything else about you, and the trouble you've lived will not rob you of your innermost, intimate part of you that only God really sees and of which you have only part understanding. That for which the first couple reached is within your grasp but not by a lie. It is a gift that is yours by the life I give you.*

"God so loved the world that he gave his one and only Son, that whoever believes in him will not perish but have eternal life" (v. 16 NIV). *You see, you will not die; you will live, and it starts now. For I have come that you may have life and have it fully, abundantly, rich and satisfying with the essentials of all that life is and needs. Even more so, it will carry you from this life, this trouble, into an even better existence with me forever.*

So God loves, and God gives. God gives God's self in a human form who lived and died for real, reversing trouble by reversing where trouble ends into what God and every created person wants—not death, but the life that fulfills Love.

That day when Jesus hung on the cross, with all its repulsive gruesomeness, could only be comprehended under this blanket of Love.

That Last Night Together

Even so, Jesus wanted to prepare his disciples, his dearest followers, of the inevitability of his death, this trouble with Jesus. He also wanted them to know that by this trouble would be the greatest expression of love. In all, though it sounded like desertion to their ears, he was telling them he'd never let go of them through the coming trouble and beyond. That last night together, he told them so many things. It was hard to hear so much of it, hard to take it all in, hard to believe.

But Jesus kept talking. He had just said that it was time to leave this place and go. But for some reason, he kept talking. The tension in the room was a weighty blend of grief, some denial, maybe even suppressed anger at what he was saying, all held in place by the exhaustion of the week. He kept saying things like being lifted on a cross even as he almost desperately called to the people to believe he was sent from God. Still, he just kept talking. Then he had said the unthinkable, that one of them, these who had followed him and learned from him for three years, would betray him. Maybe that's why he had said to Judas, "Hurry and do what you're going to do" (13:27). Judas was the treasurer who had paid for their meals and given money to the poor. Do you think he left to pay off any threat to their rabbi and themselves? Jesus kept talking.

In all the confusion, Peter declared he would die for his Lord. Jesus silenced the room when he told Peter that he would go so far as to three times deny he even knew Jesus before that very night was over. Next came some kind of talk about going away somewhere and how Jesus would send a Counselor to teach and remind his disciples of what he had said.

It was too much, how he kept talking even when he said they should be going. It was as if Jesus knew when they left that room, he never again would have the chance to tell them all he wanted. So he weaved in his thoughts, let them creep out and hold on where they would, seemingly just talk but growing into so much more.

"I am the true vine, and my Father is the gardener" (15:1 NIV). A vine. The image is one similar to what he was doing now. A vine grows, spreads out, weaves up into and among places to which it can grasp, wrap itself, become stable-tight, and then move out again. His words had been like that all night—thin trails of thought getting thicker with meaning.

Jesus fleshed out the metaphor. His Father, the one from whom he comes, is the gardener. The work of this Gardener-God is made clear from the beginning: he works to produce fruit. The gardener trains the branches on the vine, how to grow and spread out so light is available to all parts of it. The parts that impede the ability to produce fruit are removed, pruned.

Such it has been with these friends of Jesus. The message he gave them cut away at their ambitions, desires, and misconceptions of God's purpose for them. Pruning can be severe, but it's necessary for the fruit of the vine. Not all will accept being part of the vine. The separation leaves a wound on the vine like something nailed deep into flesh. Still, though severe, a necessary pruning can also be a cleansing, yielding process, as if having feet or hands washed. The health of the vine and the expected fruit must be protected from disease. Yielding to the Gardener-God's work maintains the well-being of the branches.

Jesus said that from the True Vine comes branches, and from the yield of the branches comes fruit. An interconnectedness sits in the image that belies the translations. Eight times Jesus states the importance of remaining, abiding, being joined to him. "Apart from me, you can do nothing" (v. 5). You won't know growth, he tells the ones he loves. You can't be effective. You won't have life in the abundance the Gardener-God would have for you. You won't last because you won't produce fruit. Abide, remain in, and be joined to Jesus's message of love.

To abide is to be not just a branch, an appendage, but also an integral part of the vine. By the embeddedness of the two, the branch is identified with the True Vine. Thus, in an intimate conjoining of love, the True Vine connects with its branches. Yet, this metaphor is not limited to individuals.

"Whatever you ask in my name," Jesus said, "the Father will give you" (v. 16 NIV). Not a whatever-you-want-and-it's-all-yours does he offer here.

Not a blanket giveaway is this. Throughout Jesus's words, he speaks the plural form of "you." "You" entails the interconnected, gathered believers who remain in, are joined to, and abide in the True Vine. He speaks into a future that had not yet been imagined. In the altogether growing, cleansing, pruning of the branches is a mutual desire in producing fruit of the Vine.

Jesus kept talking. His message was slowly understood as the tenuous wisps of leaves, like his thoughts, sprouted from the tips of the branch connected to the True Vine. His discourse was cloudy in its first reception, requiring multiple reexaminations as the vine sent out more branches.

Jesus kept talking. Fruit is the desire of his Gardener-God. Fruit will be taken from the vine of love and crushed into a cup from which Jesus soon poured out his life. The True Vine stared into his fate. He kept talking.

"There is no greater love than to lay down one's life for one's friends," Jesus told them (v. 3). This is the ultimate sacrifice—a life that becomes no more so that others may continue in that life and have more. The men heard this, realizing Jesus would not turn away from that fate. Immense emotion, conflicted feelings, coupled with a blessed numbness floated within them. Yet, one great question not spoken hung in the room: Does this have to be?

Jesus kept talking. His words attempted to prepare his friends for what was to come, the laying down of his own life. He knew how in the last three years they had not been altogether on board, how they had their own agendas for what their rabbi should accomplish. Soon, however, his own blood would be spilled out. On this night his words gushed, knowing they would not make sense, not until later. Then, insight, new perspectives, revelation would come. Then they would know that his death had to be.

"I have loved you even as the Father has loved me. Remain in my love" (v. 9). Some of the last words the disciples needed to get them through spoke of love. Yet were they able to know that love that Jesus expressed to them? Love, not as sentiment, not as desire or need, not as a possession of one for the other. Love as the Father loved. But more.

"Love each other in the same way I have loved you" (v. 12). The Father's love for the Son is the love the Son has for them. Love is the binding force, not dependent on mere good vibes received but on mutual, concentric interconnections. No greater love, Jesus said. Love other than this is lacking, insufficient to contain or keep close that remaining, abiding relationship of deepest intimacy. What would follow was Jesus's own example of this great Love, laying down his life for another, for the world.

But did this have to be? Why a blood sacrifice, why go into this with eyes wide open for what would happen? Why, oh God, did you not get him the heck out of there?

Because, as he said, no greater Love is there. No other understanding, example, means of showing you the depth of divine love, the go-to-any-lengths kind of love Jesus so desperately wants for those who follow him. For by that Love, they are seen and transformed from being mere disciples, followers of a rabbi, ones who serve their master. "You are my friends if you do what I command" (v. 14). They become friends. Friends of the deepest ilk and kin. Friends as they remain and abide in him. Friends as they live out this love of God and Son in life.

Love like this is sacrificial in the greatest sense, greater than understood by most. In all, not many comparatively are called to lose their lives for others. When it happens on the battlefield, the streets, by heroic actions of first responders, we bow our heads in gratefulness for their ultimate sacrifice. Still, just as grateful are we that it is not us, not our sacrifice.

Yet Jesus said, no greater Love entails laying down one's life. To do so in Love is to daily relinquish the right to oneself in character and living that follows Jesus. God knows, as do we, if we gave up our physical lives all the time, there'd be no one left among the few who might join up. Yet this kind of love—sacrificial Love, Love that lays one's life down in self-centered fulfillment—finds purpose in service for others by daily actions which live in hearts remaining, abiding, and living out that Love.

Closer to the point, to fully Love is to examine what one does in relationships not because one feels like it, wants to do it, or enjoys seeing the other pleased by it. It's the stand-alongside-another Love even if and when one's own emotional center is empty, drained, just not feeling it. The decision to Love like this is a laying down of one's life when the prospect of getting one's needs met in it seem dim.

But does this have to be? This makes one vulnerable, almost too vulnerable as it opens oneself to this kind of love. Does this have to be?

"Love each other as I have loved you," he commanded (v. 12 NIV).

But if love is only following orders, how can it be love?

Jesus gave this command to show that Love has to be. Hear this, though, as not a rigid directive but more as a plea in its strongest form. Love each other, he said, "so that you will be filled with my joy. Yes, your joy will overflow!" (v. 11).

To love, then, as Jesus loves, as God loves, is to love each other. In this, that interconnected, intimate binding of one to the other is a joy not otherwise known, not possible in the expectations of personal desire focused on oneself. It's a learned art but found in the most characteristic activity of God.

Filled with my joy, Jesus said. Yes, joy, but it's *his* kind of joy. To act decisively, sacrificially, purposely in a love that doesn't seek its own satisfaction is not an artificial love that seeks its own ends or can sink to manipulation, even abuse. Its mutuality, instead, produces a transformative love, with each person in the relationship becoming greater in love to the other. To be lifted out of oneself to become a creature of love is Jesus's purpose and brings joy. For this then, the no greater love of Jesus had to be. To that end, Jesus laid down his life for his friends.

"If you love me, obey my commandments" (14:15). *Do these not to tick off some holy checklist. Let these commandments become the deepest expression of your love for me, the center of your very soul. For my sayings will teach you to love as I love you and the entire created world.*

> Dear Jesus, if I may. If!? That's another one of those loaded words on both our parts. "If" can mean something that's conditional, or whenever, or even though, or whether (or not). "If I may" is a way of asking "Allow me." Somehow, I don't think you're asking permission in saying this. You're putting out there two things: love and rules.

Commandments may sound like orders: Do this or else. Jesus always offers a choice, though, not insisting on it, not forcing someone into it. But to see things only from your own perspective, life on your terms, is life narrowed and individualistic, self-centered even. Until you enter into another's understanding, you can't know who they really are. Required is a willingness to enter into another's understanding so as to grasp fully their viewpoint, needs, where and how they were formed into the person they are. Commandments bring protective boundaries. Prefacing or couching them in relationship to love is instructive more so than regimented. Jesus offers that choice.

This isn't anything new for Jesus's friends. They've known this since all so very long ago, far back when God gathered them as the chosen people, freeing them from oppression and guiding them through the wilderness. That guidance came in the form of other commandments—commandments designed and intended to keep them in God's love and in relationship with each other by love. Jesus summarized this law best as the greatest commandment: "You must love the Lord your God with all your heart, all your soul, and all your mind." Equally important was, "Love your neighbor as yourself" (Matthew 22:37–39).

Jesus accepts no less than a relationship of love. One can't love God without loving others, nor love others without the full love of God. Like the vine, the two are intertwined, mutually dependent on the other. To love God is to love by the examination of oneself, the knowing fully of one's strengths of body, mind, and soul. In that knowing and from that knowing, love is activated, expressed, and given to others.

"Do to others as you would like them to do for you" (Luke 6:31). Examination of self will direct you. It's a perspective of fellow humans and humanity as creatures and creations of worth—persons and peoples loved by God even as they are loved. From this, it's possible to intuitively know what to do, how to treat others with respect and honor, leveling relationships through God-inspired equality and mutual understanding.

Love of neighbor cannot be divisive or discriminatory, even with those who you cannot see on the surface as ones deserving of your love. "But to you who are willing to listen, I say, love your enemies! Do good to those who hate you. Bless those who curse you. Pray for those who hurt you" (vv. 27–28).

> Jesus, please stop this talking right there. It's been good so far. Love makes the world go round, they say. Remember the good ol' days when we had love-ins? Sweet, they were. But you go on to say things like turn the other cheek when someone hits you, if someone confiscates your coat to offer your shirt, walk that extra mile when drafted unfairly in service. That's a kind of submissiveness that permits abuse and plays into sociopathic tendencies. Come on, there are limits to everything, even love.

Well said, as far as it goes. Boundaries are important, even so much as major expressions of love. Think about "commandments" like that. Loving boundaries teach and express love which form the basis of healthy relationships. Without them, you're right; everything will disintegrate into manipulation.

Okay, love needs boundaries. We get it. Boundaries protect people from controlling and using one another. Otherwise, this becomes a statement of manipulation, more like prove you love me by obeying my commandments. A healthy love and relationship are shown by respecting boundaries. So you're saying this is how you want to be loved, how you want to be known, what you are assertively saying you want the relationship to have in it.

But note here that the major premise still holds: Treat others like you want to be treated. Enemies are those who would push, even violate, those boundaries. Jesus said to pray for them. You can't hate someone forever if you keep praying for them. Eventually, you'll learn or realize what you may not have known before, that point of mutuality from which the relationship can change. It's the beginning of love.

Finally, this Love does not permit neglect of those whom Jesus loved most dearly, the forgotten losers known as the poor and needy. In a parable of sheep and goats, Jesus made clear that when all in this world is said and done, there will be a reckoning, a time when the shepherd will separate the sheep from the goats. To the sheep is given warm welcome in the Father's kingdom. They are not there because they went to church or were known as good people in the community. This entry and acceptance are possible because they served the Father's Son. He says, "For I was hungry, and you fed me. I was thirsty, and you gave me a drink. I was a stranger, and you invited me into your home. I was naked, and you gave me clothing. I was sick, and you cared for me. I was in prison, and you visited me" (Matthew 25:35–36).

Those represented as sheep haven't a clue about this. "Lord, when did we ever see you hungry . . . thirsty . . . a stranger . . . naked . . . sick or in prison . . . ?" (vv. 37–39). In a revelation of himself, Jesus confides, "When you did it to one of the least of these . . . , you were doing it to me!" (v. 40). His love and the loving actions of those who love him are always watching for those who most need to feel and realize that love. This love is given in provision of daily need and service in their places of trouble. To act toward others in giving and sacrifice, to love as Jesus loved—as a crucified Love that changes and reverses one's need to protect oneself in exchange of purpose—is to know, to see Jesus for how and why he enters the trouble of those he loves.

Love follows its Lover. Jesus is saying, *know why I came and what I have taught you. Make your life and your relationships among those who can do nothing for you, who do not have power or wealth or status. Take care of the children, for their kind of faith is the kind in which I take most joy. Have persons close to you who know trouble of body, mind, and soul. Be among the oppressed, the sick, the outcast, the losers of this world who will only bring complications and trouble for you. That is how you love me.*

Love me knowing your money is not what I value in you and thus has little value to me as your Lover. Be ready to walk away from it or give it all away if that's what I ask of you. Count it as a blessing that is not for your benefit but in knowing how to use it to love me by loving those I love with it, that is, the people nobody else wants. Rid your life of those attitudes about money which bring you trouble.

Love God and your neighbor, Jesus declared as the greatest commandments, the summary of the entire law. *Do not oppress others with your laws as you have done with women in your social strata. They, like all persons, were not made for your use and pleasure and servitude but to learn from me at my feet, to anoint me with extravagance, to speak and teach of my healing love in loud praise. Keep holiness in your relationships, remembering that the highest relationship of marriage is the one that will require of you the most work and sometimes the most trouble. Like the water at the wedding, be ready to be changed, to pour out your life in sacrifice, and to be better persons because of it.*

Don't misrepresent my love for you, Jesus cautions. *Yes, my love for you means I want the best for you. When trouble destroys your life, takes from you that which robs you of my best purposes in creating you, I can reverse the trouble and restore you. But realize this: when I do, and I don't do it often enough from your point of understanding, it ultimately has nothing to do with making you happy. Expect that just as bread was broken for a multitude to be fed, so will you be broken as you feed my sheep. Still, in that brokenness you will find your best blessing, your joy and mine, as your life is given for others.*

Furthermore, Jesus reminds his followers, *I reverse trouble only for one reason: to show you who I am. I am not like you or any others who claim to know God. I am God in the form of God's Son. I feed people, heal people, and preach so that you may have a glimpse into who I am and how much I love you. It was for Love that I came to live among you for a while in your trouble; it was for Love that I allowed the trouble of the world to annihilate me; and it was for Love that I reversed trouble in what the grave holds. In my revelation of myself in resurrected form, others witnessed to my love, proclaiming that trouble is not the final story. They did so and do so because I remain here among them and you by my Spirit. For I love you so much, I cannot even now leave you.* "And be sure of this: I am with you always, even to the end of the age" (Matthew 28:20).

Further Provocations for Your Consideration

1. Jesus said to love your enemies. Loving implies forgiveness. Does forgiveness erase consequences?

_____

_____

_____

_____

_____

_____

_____

2. What conflict, if any, is there between loving an enemy and upholding justice?

_____

_____

_____

_____

_____

3. Love God and love your neighbor are the greatest commandments. Does this kind of love erase judgment? Can there be love without accountability?

_____

_____

_____

_____

_____

4. Again, loving enemies implies forgiveness. Does forgiveness include reconciliation? Is reconciliation always achievable?

_____

_____

_____

_____

5. Jesus's miracles were not just for the benefit of those who received them but also to identify who he was as the Son of God. Is this fully accurate? Where is love, or at least compassion, in this part of his story? How were his miracles misunderstood? In the same way, how are prayers used to "serve God in an advisory capacity?" Yet if prayers are not answered as requested, is this still a reflection of God's Love?

_____

_____

_____

_____

_____

_____

6. How does John 3:16 state the fulfillment of God's Love?

_____

_____

_____

_____

_____

_____

_____

9

The Denouement

"Mary!" (John 20:16).

She turned quickly, surprised that the gardener knew her name. She had been crying so vehemently that she couldn't see clearly, hadn't even seen him there behind her.

Three days earlier, along with his mother and the other women who supported him, Mary Magdalene watched Jesus know his final trouble—the torture of a cross. The women had clung to each other as he choked his last words through pain. His burial had to be a fast one, before the sun set beginning the Sabbath, ancient laws again encroaching on her life. In the numbness of grief, she knew what she must do. Early that morning, even before dawn, she had prepared and carried the cloths and spices to wipe clean and honor Jesus's butchered body.

When she heard her name this time, abruptly her heart stopped and leapt. There had been no one who had ever spoken her name, called her name, like Jesus did. Now her Healer and Savior stood before her, all trouble reversed, drained, and erased from his being. He was alive! What he had promised, Jesus offered now to her and any others who would hear their name called.

Do You Believe This?

For the others, the story was drastically different. When the disciples heard the good news, they didn't believe it. Don't blame them. People today are no different. To be honest, it helps to know they didn't know what to believe. It helps a lot, for if the report that went out to others was that the women were believed, who would believe it? They were women after all. Men didn't accept their testimony as reliable. And if these former fishermen had swallowed what the women said hook, line, and sinker, it'd be pretty evident that their story was falsified. The men didn't believe it, plain and simple.

Then, Jesus suddenly appeared in the same room as the fearful, shattered disciples.

> Hey, weren't these the guys who'd heard Jesus talk more than once about giving up his life for others? Still, you couldn't expect this. Jesus, brutally tortured until dead on a cross, expired for three days, and just like that, there he is in the same room, alive and well. Even the reports about the women at the tomb say they were scared out of their wits. The men thought they were delirious. Now their minds were being blown as well. Yeah, it's hard to wrap your head around. Had to be a zombie of some sort. Nope, don't blame them. We're with them.

Jesus was back, alive, well, resurrected from the dead as the saying goes. What would be anyone's thought? Walking dead, for sure. That's all they could think of, reverting back to some kind of pagan superstition. Jesus understood their reaction. He was real but from a new kind of reality. His work with them was certainly cut out for him.

First, he spoke words familiar to them: "Peace be with you" (v. 20). Shalom. On the one hand, it's like saying, "Hey, guys. I'm here. Everything's cool." But they also know his kingdom as one of peace. Peace, not as absence of conflict, but peace that calms the soul-storms, clarifies with a new sense or vision, unites in purpose to God and each other, empowers with strength of presence and being. He offered this peace to them.

Jesus appeared to them, and now he was talking just like he used to. The disciples were still petrified. This wasn't going to be an easy sell. Jesus got right down to it. "Why are your hearts filled with doubt?" Minds need proof, an experiential, empirical understanding of existence, design, and method. Jesus rolled up his sleeves and kicked off his sandals. "Look at my hands. Look at my feet. You can see that it's really me. Touch me and make sure that I am not a ghost, because ghosts don't have bodies, as you see that I do" (Luke 24:38–39). *Look. Touch. I'm a physical body. I'm real as life.*

So, that's a good one. But would it last? Jesus was not there and then suddenly appears there. Real bodies don't do that. Is this what it's like being drawn into something that's beyond weird?

This isn't weird. Ghosts may look like what they were when alive, but ghosts don't have physical functions. The disciples were still doubting, though something like hope was stirring too as they also felt joy and wonder. Jesus asked them for something to eat and scarfed down some broiled fish (vv. 41–43). He's hungry. Why not? It's been three days since that last supper, so to speak. There was something so natural and alive in him. They watched and recalled what they knew him to be.

Yet, in the role they knew him best, for the role by which they first followed him, Jesus spoke as their rabbi, their teacher. This is the Jesus they knew, the Jesus who called them by saying "Come and see." For three years he had instructed them, expanding the ancient writings and commandments God had given their ancestors. He showed them again in the words of the prophets how the Messiah would suffer, die, and rise again on the third day. This they could remember and use to piece together the events of the last few days. By reminding them, Jesus opened their minds to this new reality, this privilege they had to glimpse not mere life after death, not just a resuscitation back to what was, but a translation into having a closer presence in the love of God. Eternal life is the catchall term for it.

Want a better explanation? Go for it, but good luck with that. Herein is the journey of faith, that place of tension between doubt and belief. What happens after death is a huge question. Yet efforts to approximate it to what is already known is refusal to enter into the mystery of it, a grounding of logical proofs that negate wonder.

That Jesus lived and died on a cross is a verifiable fact. Resurrection is the pivotal place of doubt and belief. Yet doubt is where faith begins. Everyone who first heard that Jesus was alive responded first with doubt. Can't blame them, right? They went from too-good-to-be-true, to can't-believe-it-is-true, to this wonder that it might be true. Courageous souls float in wonder, the position between doubt and belief. It's not denial as opposed to blind acceptance. It's feeling the pull of not understanding the hows of doubt for an exchange of acceptance in the whys of belief. Trust, then, is the operative part of faith, the not knowing but somehow accepting.

Jesus blessed the disciples in his greeting of shalom—peace in lives that can carry this tension of wonder and bring a witness of how far God will go to bring restoration. That someone would die for a good cause is believable, but how someone could come back from death for the cause of transforming love is the stretch, where trouble sits hard. Do you believe this?

To further beg the question, though, where is the stronger faith? In the one totally convinced, or in the one who can't explain away but somehow accepts? "You are witnesses," Jesus said (v. 48). *Turn to me, accept me and my life offering for you. Be restored and reconciled to God in love. And wonder with peace.*

Doubting Believers

Resurrection? Eternal life? Another way of promising "You won't die"? Just by buying into what you said and did two millennia ago? I don't know. Oh my, Jesus, you're such a stretch; it's unbelievable.

Unbelievable is right. It doesn't take modern thought, science, and developed worldviews to come to that conclusion. Jesus knew it then, even before the story was complete. And he knew it from one of his oldest, closest friends, the one whose destiny was to prepare the way for his coming.

John, his cousin, son of Elizabeth and Zechariah, had been Jesus's greatest advocate. Though John had a great following as preacher and prophet in his own right, his message of repentance—turning from and reversing one's life in the direction of God—had garnered many who offered themselves to be lowered and raised in river water. Though he was being compared to, and some thought he actually was, the prophet Elijah, there was a bottom to John's belief as well. A life preaching in the desert wasn't so much trouble for him as being in the pit of Herod's jail. Arrested and knowing his life was at the mercy of a sick tetrarch, John had to ask himself if this life of God and following a messianic figure was worth it. Or rather, John had to have an answer to help with that question, "Do you believe this?"

John's followers were sent to Jesus to ask him this question: "Are you the Messiah we've been expecting . . . ?" (7:19). *Are you more than a preacher and prophet like me? Are you more than one sent by God but one who is God and with God, the Son of God? Should we still look for someone else?*

Even in his cell, John had heard what Jesus had been doing. Messages and miracles fought trouble with hope, and when one sees hope fulfilled, the hopeless ask if this could be real. There's no guarantee that it will be an easy road attached if you listen to his *Come and see. Follow me. I'll make you fishers of men (people) or more than you ever thought you'd be.* So if you're one of those who gets slammed for doing what he asks, you've got to confront this troublemaker for the answer that will determine your soul: Are you for real?

There's no record of Jesus weeping in this scenario, but maybe he could have. His connection with John went back to the womb when their mothers had communed with each other about angelic revelations and more. In John's arms, Jesus had been raised from the water to hear the divine affirmation, "This is my dearly loved Son, who brings me great joy" (Matthew 3:17). Jesus's baptism led to both of them knowing what their destinies' design would be. Jesus faced the trouble he brought with one who was supposed to share his good news. Still, what kind of good news can you give to the guy who would die by the hand of Herod, an evil kind of troublemaker, an extension of your own antithesis? Dear Jesus, will you weep now?

Sometimes all doubt needs is to be reminded of what it already knows, has seen, and has heard. It's truth not cloaked in high thoughts or mystical sayings. It simply affirms what is. "Go back to John and tell him what you have heard and seen," Jesus said. "The blind see, the lame walk, those with leprosy are cured, the deaf hear, the dead are raised to life" (11:4–5). Yes, John, Jesus is the expected Messiah. We know this because lives are changed and trouble is reversed. *I have seen and touched and spoken away that which attacks the body to get to the soul. But this is not the only miracle or the best miracle I have brought to this hurting, troubled world.* "Good News is being preached to the poor" (v. 5). *The greatest reversal, the greatest miracle is a life that is turned from its inward trouble, needs, desires, and purposes to one that is turned to God and God in me.*

"I am the way, the truth, and the life" (John 14:6), Jesus told those closest to him on the night before he met his trouble. "The words I speak are not my own, but my Father who lives in me does his work through me. Just believe that I am in the Father and the Father is in me." Then, likely knowing they always needed more, he added, "Or at least believe because of the work you have seen me do" (vv. 10–11).

"Good news to the poor" had been promised long ago by the prophet Isaiah (Isaiah 61:1). Jesus understood that John would also remember the second part, the part Jesus doesn't say and leaves out, how "captives will be released and prisoners will be freed" (v. 1). The bad news was, this wouldn't happen for John.

Jesus knew that John was like everyone else. When push comes to shove, when trouble must be acknowledged and accepted that it will do its worst, you must have something on which to hold. You must have a way not only to cope but also to get through it even to the bitter end. You need that promise stated and reminded from its source, "You won't die."

Jesus promises, *I will reverse it all by what I show you in myself.* The trouble must be faced and doubt silenced by not only resurrection and reversal in lives lived but also by the one who asked the question, "Do you believe this?" Going through a personal physical death and reversing it in himself had to be accomplished for anyone to answer in the affirmative.

Gently then, Jesus's last message and word to John is, "blessed is any person who does take offense at Me" (Matthew 11:6 NASB). Both he and John had known offense. The religious hierarchy did not afford them any status of position or education. John and Jesus did not preach solely in the sacred places of synagogue or temple but along rivers and deserts, in homes, and on hillsides. Their followers were a rough band of men and women, some of questionable repute. The people loved both prophets because of the hope they realized through forgiveness in the kingdom of God, a place where they were not oppressed by legalism or monetary greed. For this, these prophets/preachers had been dismissed since the hope they gave lay not in political or military power but in a grace and love given to even the most low and poor and those who would serve the childlike and the losers with all they had.

John had known this maybe better than any other. Jesus now was saying, *Accept my presence and the trouble it has brought you. Remember my teaching that day on a hillside, "Blessed are the poor in spirit . . . those who mourn . . . the gentle . . . the merciful . . . the peacemakers." Blessed are "those who hunger and thirst for justice," "those whose hearts are pure," those who are persecuted, and especially those who find trouble because they believe in me (Matthew 5:3–12). Trouble does not last, cannot find its way into the eternity I offer.* God reverses and restores and blesses those who believe him.

John's question about Jesus's identity was not an isolated one. On another day, a frantic father came to Jesus about his seemingly possessed, likely epileptic, son. His plea came from the empty bottom of his soul, "Have mercy on us and help us, if you can." "'If I can?'" Jesus reiterated. "Anything is possible if a person believes" (Mark 9:22–23). In other words, *Do you believe this? Do you believe that I can reverse and restore bodies and souls? Do you believe when I say, You will not die?*

In probably the most honest, candid, and revealing declaration of faith ever made, this desperate father instantly cried out, "I do believe, but help me overcome my unbelief!" (v. 24). He had no hope but still asked, daring to hope but not knowing, believing but questioning, asking and waiting to see what God could do, if God would, stretched to unfair extremes by faith colliding with trouble. Jesus healed this man's son, and there were so many other miracles to prove he was from God.

Still another doubter had struggled, this one even closer to Jesus. Thomas, one of the Twelve, had seen it all, had one time even promised to die with Jesus. But when trouble brought a cross to confront, all confidence of belief evaporated. Thomas, too, needed the miracle, to see for himself that Jesus who was unmistakably dead now lived. He had to see the scars in the hands and feet of Jesus's living body. When Jesus stood before him in flesh and blood reality, Thomas exclaimed, "My Lord and my God!" (John 20:28). He knew beyond belief that what Jesus had said he would do was accomplished. "You will not die" was for all who accepted and assented to that renewed, reversed, abundant, forever life forever that was in Jesus, the one who faced down death with death and came back from it.

Yet, in this scene that contains our chorus, we also hear yet another blessing meant for those who live beyond this time and these words: God's blessing is extended to all. Jesus acknowledged to Thomas, "You believe because you have seen me." But there are those who perhaps have even more of a blessing than a physical revelation. To those who did not know Jesus then and even more so to all throughout the world who would come later, Jesus said, "Blessed are those who believe without seeing me" (v. 29). Blessed are those who have not had the benefit of miracles. Miracles help some, but those who come to believe without them very likely have the greatest miracle of all—the miracle of a faith with assurance in the promise, "You will not die."

The irony of how Jesus had asked this could not have been lost on Peter days later. He, with some of the other disciples, had gone fishing the night before, and like the first time he met Jesus, their nets were empty. The figure on the shore was dimly lit in the just beginning dawn, but he urged them to cast their nets one more time. Like the first time, the net filled with fish beyond its capacity to hold them all. Peter immediately swam ashore, knowing again it was Jesus who was calling him. Breakfast was made, fish and bread bringing memory of that other miracle of provision, and once again Jesus became their servant in nourishment with food and grace (21:2–14).

After breakfast, separate from the others, Jesus called him, "Simon son of John" (v. 15). His words must have thrown Peter once again back to that first time Jesus had said his given name, but his calling also had given him a new name, Cephas (or Peter, meaning "rock"; 1:42). Given his piles of failures the last few years, the name Simon may have sounded like a rebuke, for Peter had been less than rock-steady in his faith. Like that time the disciples were caught in a storm on the water, Peter had been the one to sink when he looked at the high waves rather than on Jesus walking on the water (Matthew 14:22–33). Jesus had known how bad it would get, for he prayed for Peter's faith even before Peter denied him late that last night (Luke 22:32). Sure, Peter had been the one to answer another one of his questions, "Who do you say that I am?" with "You are the Messiah" (Mark 8:29). Wouldn't that declaration of Jesus's identity have been enough?

Yet, on this morning, not once but three times Jesus pressed him with the question, "Do you love me?" (John 21:15–17). Maybe the repetition was to help dispel Peter's guilt over repeatedly denying that he knew Jesus

just when the trouble really escalated with Jesus's arrest. Peter's bold declaration of Messiah was canceled that dark night in the courtyard outside the
high priest's house. A servant girl had accused Peter of being a follower. His
next words held more than what he said: "I don't even know him!" (Luke
22:57). To all who heard it, it was a clear denial that he had followed Jesus.
But in Peter's soul, it cried out that the Jesus he followed was not the Messiah he thought Jesus was but instead a Messiah that would bring deadly
trouble upon himself. So now the questions had to be asked for the sake of
Peter's troubled soul.

Even more so, it was troubling in the way Jesus asked for that love.
"Simon son of John, do you love me more than these?" (John 21:15). *More
than these brothers with whom you have followed me since that first day on
another beach?* Gathered there were James and John, Nathanael, Philip,
Andrew, even Thomas. All of them had been through so much. Today
seemed like a chance for them to start over again. *Simon, son of John, will
you start over again, follow me again? But I need to know, do you love me more
than these?* The Love Jesus required was a Love that would leave everything
behind again, to leave one's net and all that is held vital in life. It was a
God-consuming Love that meant nothing could be in front of it, not one's
security and safety in life nor one's understanding of all God meant nor
even one's right to oneself.

> Even our deepest cares and good hopes have to be put
> aside? Love you more, you ask? Acknowledging you as Son
> of God, seeing/believing you raised your whole body from a
> grave isn't enough? You do want it all, don't you? You never
> stop with the asking, do you?

No, he doesn't. Jesus's trouble and the trouble he brings are deeper than
what reasonably should be required. Jesus had faced trouble by sacrifice;
here he now asked Peter to do the same. Jesus asked him for a return of the

unconditional love that God had for Peter and all who followed Jesus, what became known as *agape* Love.

"Yes, Lord . . . you know I love you" (v. 15). Peter means it. Or at least as much as he can mean it. *Yes, Lord, I love you for I know you as the one who is closest to me, who has known me better than myself and has raised me to more than I'd ever be without you. I follow you and hold you as close to me as my own brother.* This is the friendship love called *phileo* love, again as understood by Greek culture.

True, Peter knew he could not face life after all he'd known these past three years or so, especially in the last weeks, not without Jesus, trouble and all. And true as well, Jesus was not going to let him go. This conversation did not have to take place with just Peter among the others there that day. But it did, and Peter was to learn that the one who called him Rock was going to make sure he was solid. Jesus meant to complete this reversal fully in Peter and anyone who would follow him.

"If you love me, obey my commandments," he had said (14:15). Now Jesus completed it with a specific directive: "Feed my lambs" (21:15). *Take care of those who need me, need my provision not only for body but also for soul, who reverse their lives and follow me as I asked you that first day by this very lake.*

You would think Jesus's point had been made. Troubling it can be, but Jesus never gives up asking and calling. A second time, Jesus asked Peter not only *if* but *how* Peter loved him. And again, Peter's response was the same (v. 16).

> We can relate. God, I love you as much as I can love, love for you and what you are in your Son, Jesus. I love you for what you have taught me about you and what you have done in my life. For when I follow you, my world is better for it. You show me how to avoid bringing trouble upon myself through negative choices, and you show me how to serve others in their trouble. Isn't that enough? Why ask that I love you more than these, the lives you have given me to share with you?

Jesus understands. Peter has been through a lot, and the trouble he's known has worn him hard. Maybe there's only so much a person can give, only so much you can ask of someone.

"Take care of my sheep," Jesus told him once more.

Yet again, Jesus asked, "Simon son of John, do you love me?" This third time, Jesus instead asked for what he knew Peter could give—a love that comes from a dedicated life as a soldier fulfills marching orders from a high command. It's not necessarily a love uniting desire with message and mission, but it's a step forward. Full union with God would come another day. Peter was "grieved" that Jesus had asked him three times—grieved in the need of Jesus's emphasis and grieved that he could only give so much. But his God Loved him even now just the way he was. Another day, Jesus told him, when old and no longer grasping to control life, Peter would meet trouble in a sacrifice that honored his Lord. But for now, Jesus gave Peter a task that he could live into. "Follow me" (21:19).

"Feed my sheep." *For Peter and all those who will take on this trouble in the world, feed my sheep. Feed them with love, feed their basic needs out of the resources I have provided you, feed them with respect and wholeness and these words I have given you. Feed them not with approval for all they say they want but with love that attends their deepest need and desire.* Tell them that the trouble with Jesus reverses all they are for what all they were meant to live, a life that meets the trouble of today by abundant living through the Love of God and neighbor and the confidence that life in Jesus ends with no trouble because you will not die.

I am leaving you with a gift—peace of mind and heart.
And the peace I give is a gift the world cannot give.
So don't be troubled or afraid.
—John 14:27

Further Provocations for Your Consideration

1. "Courageous souls float in wonder, the position between doubt and belief. It's not denial as opposed to blind acceptance. It's feeling the pull of not understanding the hows of doubt for an exchange of acceptance in the whys of belief." How does the tension in wonder enhance faith?

    _____

    _____

    _____

2. "What happens after death is a huge question. Yet efforts to approximate it to what is already known is refusal to enter into the mystery of it, a grounding of logical proofs that negate wonder." Does the need for verifiable, logical understanding detract from faith? Or does the lack of it feed into faith? Explain.

    _____

    _____

    _____

3. The man with the epileptic son confessed to Jesus, "I do believe, but help me overcome my unbelief!" What does this statement reveal about faith?

    _____

    _____

    _____

4. John the Baptist, Thomas, even Peter, all had their struggles accepting Jesus's ministry and/or his resurrection. How does their struggle reveal a fear of what their acceptance or belief of Jesus's life and message would mean for them?

_____

_____

_____

_____

5. "Jesus opened their minds to this new reality, this privilege they had to glimpse not mere life after death, not just a resuscitation back to what was, but a translation into having a closer presence in the love of God. 'Eternal life' is the catchall term for it." What is your own way of understanding Jesus's resurrection?

_____

_____

_____

_____

6. "I am the resurrection and the life. Anyone who believes in me will live, even after dying. Everyone who lives in me and believes in me will never ever die. Do you believe this?" (John 11:25–26). What's your answer?

_____

_____

_____

_____

10

The Epilogue

"I am the resurrection and the life. Anyone who believes in me will live, even after dying. Everyone who lives in me and believes in me will never ever die. Do you believe this?" (John 11:25–26).

Our hero's recorded words and actions are contained in four short writings. Whatever has been said about him in derision or proclaimed in theological discourse gives answer to "Do you believe this?" For two thousand years, this is the question that is answered by lives who either outright affirm or deny him. Even so, the real trouble lies with those like the persons in that first garden who want it all.

Still, though the times and places of Jesus's life have passed into antiquity, our chorus continues to speak its challenges and doubts, searching for a place in Jesus's story. This voice is heard in the depths of troubled seeking souls and in the hard constructs of religion and the intricacies of philosophy. Its heart cries its pain in the genres of art, music, and literature. By science, psychology, and education, it seeks to explain its still unsatisfied self. Through political, military, and humanitarian endeavors alongside technological advances, it promotes change but cannot find stability. In all, the chorus voices both personal and existential focus, purpose, and maybe even divine significance in its life of trouble.

The Eternal Question

"Do you believe this?" Eternity rests on its answer. Our chorus finds its place as not only observer and sometimes player in the story, but also with contemporary voices that still utter their trouble only to be answered with the trouble Jesus means for them.

Give me what I want. And understand, I want it all and I want it for me. It's everyone for her or himself out there.

I'll give a little, but only enough so I can feel kind of good about it, especially when you fools think I'm so wonderful for doing it.

Don't make me change. Forget your reversals. It took a lot for me to get where I am, and don't think I'm going to give it up for some kind of cross like you got to carry.

No, love me as I am. That is, just go along with what I am. Don't think I'm going to exchange who I am for what you want me to be.

If you're not going to take care of me, what good are you to me? That's what you're supposed to do, and you should do it the way I want it. Fix my stuff the way I want it done.

Punish others, but don't judge me. Sure, there are a lot of really bad and wrong things in the world. Just don't lay any of it on me. Really, I didn't make any of this up, so don't think I've started it. And if I get angry about all this trouble, don't blame me for what I do about it.

I'll find God on my own and explain God in my own way. If some want to follow you and get crucified for it, that's their business. Just don't push yourself on me and think I'm going to live my life as you want it. Honestly, you are sometimes just over the top with all you think I should do. Forget it. My kind of God isn't going to put me through this.

Yeah, that's right. Let me be my own God; give me control. That's what I want most anyway. From the way I see it, we all wind up in the same sad state anyway and that's dead. So if I'm going to die, I'll be in charge with whatever time I've got. You keep your losers, and I'll keep my money. I'll treat women the way I want, and I can be the kind of woman who knows how to use what she's got to get what she wants. Morality? Only when it's for my gain.

So you are the great miracle worker? You know, if you made all this, then why are things so messed up? To make it right would be the real miracle. Then again, you don't really want to do it because we would be better off. No, you keep things screwed and only make a miracle every now and then so you can get credit as the Great Almighty. It makes us wonder if that's what all this trouble is really for, just to make you look good. There are enough narcissists out there. I'm not going to be grateful for another one.

As for your love, who needs the kind you have to give. Sure, you say you loved enough to die for me. But that only means you want me to die to myself in exchange. One good death deserves another? Jesus, did you drink too much of that good wine you made at the wedding? No wonder you got in so much trouble. Don't think I'd ever want to spend any kind of eternity with the likes of you.

The world spins and rocks trouble, resists by trying to beat death even as it hastens the inevitable, but the question doesn't go away: "Do you believe this?"

Our drama has ended but is not complete. The tragic hero has been honored and revered, and his fortune turned to tragedy. His flaw is not in character or moral weakness or misjudgment. He speaks directly into the human character and culture, two thousand years ago as well as now. For revealing too much of who we are and who he is, he riled those who would have the most to lose and for that he was killed. Had Jesus lived in this day and age, he would have met the same conflict and fate.

Our chorus, the voices in the world today, know the same desires as the couple in that ancient garden. To be in control of one's life, to live as one wants and be as one wants, to "be like God" and have the freedom to exercise one's choice in life is no different and has not changed in all of the earth's ages. The ultimate quest is for this choice to go on, to have it all and for it never to end. "You will not die," in whatever state we imagine this, is the world's pursuit. For if all that limited us were eradicated—disease, poverty, war, aging processes, oppression—we could not only eliminate the anguish these and other disasters achieve, but we ultimately could stop death, not just delay it. So our chorus hopes to someday say,

> We do not need a God. We do not need a Savior. We are God. We will not die!

Still, the trouble with Jesus proposes another choice. Certainly, none would ask that advancements which improve and save lives be halted. Yet, that's not the point. Rather than an inward focus on oneself, personally or collectively, Jesus asks for a reversal, a turning from our natural inclination and common sense to an embrace in Love offered for all creation. And yet, the historical record is such that humans want control, not only over their own lives but also over others. The tendency to dominate never leaves no matter how enlightened and progressive our motivations. From there, the power it feeds is only a few steps away from wanting all influence, command, dominion, supremacy. Hegemony infects everyone in some way. In the end, people do anything to get it. So it was, when Jesus moved among the losers of his time, called children to his side, recognized women as daughters of faith, expanded his mission to peoples and places not of his own, and called for an upheaval of wealth that serves others, he spoke trouble to that dominance.

What Jesus offers is cathartic, just as any drama would portray, though not as a mere symbol or scapegoat. The reversal he offers is to release the human needs spanning basic survival through self-actualization to him, to identify with him on a cross absorbing it all, ending the burdens, the trouble of this life, and reversing it for a new kind of life. He lived and died by this. By asking the question "Do you believe this?," Jesus offers not just revitalization but new creation, a new kind of living and loving.

Jesus troubles many. His life and words from long ago challenge those who follow him and those who reject him. From some perspectives, following his example has meant the downfall of many persons who claim him as Lord, knowing persecution, maybe ostracized by culture canceling. To not pander to the powerful but to stand with the losers, the oppressed, and the defenseless sometimes is determined to be beyond practical practice. Then again, even churches have defended their property over people. Likewise, secular social policy efforts claim to help others. But to give up everything, to sell all you have to give to the poor is purportedly nonsensical according to good financial planners and the desire to always want more. What's desired is some kind of middle or a medium.

The chorus raises the protest:

Follow. Yes, we'll follow Jesus for some things, or at least assent to his wise teachings on love, but we don't want this to be too much trouble. Don't make any of us change or reverse what we do.

The trouble is, though, that Jesus's words still call.

The trouble with Jesus is that "Follow me" means to give our all to him. "Those of you who do not give up everything you have cannot be my disciples" (Luke 14:33 NIV). See, the trouble with Jesus is that's what he did. More so, he told his disciples to do the same. The purpose was to ensure that nothing held a soul back from complete surrender to who one was for and what one would become by following Jesus. And in doing so, he literally gave his life without resistance to the trouble the worst of the world in hanging on to itself could design: a bloody and excruciatingly painful death on a cross. That's what he did. Death by sacrifice.

Tension in the Trouble

One would think that God could accomplish the plan a better way. But that wouldn't have happened. To preach love is one thing, but to do what one cannot do for oneself is how Love is known. By dying a death which gives up all control is to die a death that shows Jesus Loves so much that he would do what can't be done by us, on our own. Acceptance of this sacrifice occurs by belief in the one who is greater in Love than can be otherwise experienced. Therefore, Jesus exchanged his place as God for identity as human. His living water became wine, and wine became his blood.

Wine becomes blood when it is poured out; his life's cup was emptied. Yet in drinking that wine, accepting his sacrifice, life is better—better in a life lived and better in a kind of life never realized or possible before. If Jesus only had died on that cross or by any other means for that matter, and no other change had happened, the wine would not have been better. It would have left a sickening, bitter taste and feeling in the bottom of all souls. "Are you the Messiah?" would have had to be answered in the negative. This trouble would not be worth it.

Wine poured out became his blood, and that blood was Love. Love poured out makes all things possible, for nothing is impossible with God. Love poured out is life-changing, reversing, fully realized in making the impossible happen, "You will not die," and bringing new life. Jesus asks any who would believe in him, follow him fully in being like him, to take on this new kind of life. The trouble with Jesus is that he asks for all because he gave it all.

More so, the trouble with Jesus is that he fulfilled that new life. In physical form, he came out of his grave, spoke with his followers, revealed his scars. Our hero has lived and died and now lives on. But rather than acting out ancient patterns of drama, the wishes of the world for mythological heroes to portray, Jesus is the fulfillment of the sense that life holds more than numbered days and death.

Okay, we get it. Jesus was a real person. Believe it as fact. These reports of him written by his followers and those who worked closely with them tell us of this Love which he preached, lived for, and dearly wanted for people to accept. Again, accepted. People need to have that in their lives which raises them from self-centered animals of which the fittest survive. Human history notes that much. Jesus gives the best example, the best teaching of that which can reverse who we are to the best we have in us to be. The fact he was willing to sacrifice his life on a cross, to die by what you call the worst of the world and not back down, compromise, or restate his message in any way may have brought trouble but also was the exclamation point on how he lived by it. We only hope we can be like that.

But still, there's this final trouble that's still hard to swallow. "I am the resurrection and the life. Anyone who believes in me will live, even after dying. Everyone who lives in me and believes in me will never ever die. Do you believe this?" (John 11:25–26). Now, before we end this, let's examine what it means to "live again." Furthermore, is the resurrection really that Jesus walked out of his cave-grave?

Be fair about it. These same reports say Jesus even told his disciples the night he was leaving them that he would send them a Helper, a Counselor, what today they call the Holy Spirit (15:26; 16:5–7). Now hold on to that. It's plausible that's actually what Jesus meant all those times he said he would die but be raised after three days. Whatever happened to his physical dead body and its disposal you can ascribe to whatever conspiracy theory you like. The point being what the women, the disciples, all those who say they "saw" Jesus after he died was not a physically risen-from-the-dead Jesus but the essence of Jesus in his Spirit form. So let's leave it at that. This is how Jesus "resurrected" and what he meant by saying that those who believe in him live again, have eternal life, will not perish.

No one ever said this was easy. No one ever said it makes sense as far as we can understand. Did you notice the premise of this book is trouble?

> Why, oh God, why is this so hard? Why do you take us and stretch us and make us give up so much?

Understood. But we're not done yet. Follow this, if you will, for a moment.

Whenever someone dies who is dearly loved and had an immense impact on our lives, thoughts of him or her live on in our hearts and minds. Years can go by, and even if the hard grief is worked through, loss finds its place so lives can go on, not altogether without them even if not physically with them. Indeed, every day there can be something to bring these loved ones to mind as we remember them, even talk to them. The human brain is very adept at replacing, finding what it needs, maybe even "seeing" this loved one in dreams, glimpses of persons passing by who resemble the lost one, a sensing that he or she is near. Given who Jesus was and what he meant to so many as he lived and loved others, this would be understandable in how they would report the days following his death. Furthermore, it's not to be denied his followers were traumatized in those last days. All they had thought and believed would happen was killed on a cross along with Jesus. Their mental states were sorely hurting.

So when his body, no less than on the third day as he'd talked about, apparently disappeared, maybe grief took over. That's not to discount all the reports of persons seeing Jesus. They did see him, but there is the thought that what they saw was Jesus in the form of Spirit. That would mean Jesus appearing at the same time to many of them, as with Thomas or Peter and the rest of them on that beach. In their hurting, grieving minds, Jesus could have seemed so real it was as if he was alive again. And Jesus was real, but in a new way—as a spirit, not as a body. That's one way of thinking about it.

> Yep, that's one way. It's a combination of all things we like: common sense coupled with what we'd like to believe. The

story has reached its finale, shut the book, take a deep breath, and move on. Some of us can believe this much. We're fine.

Except.

How does the belief that Jesus's spirit continued in the lives of his believers differ from that of anyone else who has died and is remembered dearly? Oh yeah, Jesus has an advantage over the average dead person. He had a book, what some call a holy book written about him. It's a good story with all the drama, heroic figures, flawed people, even the very presence of personified evil set in a conflict, climax, and ending that wraps up everything so you can feel good about it. So, he gets to be remembered a lot longer than most of the rest of us ever will be. But to limit Jesus as merely a historical man or as almost a mythological figure is to kill him off better than the cross ever did.

Now certainly Jesus was a good man, a holy man some would say. How he challenged his followers and his world is just as big a challenge in today's contemporary culture. He meant it when he said you must be born again. You must be willing to start over, to change, to reverse all you thought was right and good and needed. Again, you must have a renewal in your heart, soul, and mind, and that renewal is based in love.

Troubled by Love

So what's the problem there? If love is what you're aiming for, if love is your highest and loftiest idea of what life can achieve, you'll get good press out of it, but you'll die out like the flower-loving hippies of the last century. Hopes, intentions, and aspirations won't last without power behind them, and the kind of Love Jesus preached, promoted, and passed on had power like never seen before. That power was sourced from the very Love of God—a Love that wants to enter into the lives of all individuals. It is like but is so much more than a cosmic force floating in the universe. It's so personal that God had to show up in the form of his own creation, that of a human, to be fully revealed and understood as that Love. Humanity's attempts at love have been good efforts at best, but face it, if that kind of human-based love were really effective, we wouldn't have the problems, the trouble we have today. That trouble needs a bigger Love than what you or I can muster up in ourselves. Jesus brought that kind of Love.

How did he bring it?

He talked about it a lot.

So what? So have other great persons.

He gave glimpses of it in the miracles he did, not to just fix things in the moment but also to show that power of love in changing lives.

Fine. The progress of humanity has likewise done what many thought impossible, like walking on the moon and flying to Mars, to developing a vaccine against a global pandemic in record time. We do it for the betterment of the world. So what? How's that different than Jesus's instantaneous miracles, if you put any belief in them?

The betterment of the world is certainly an expression of love, a belief that humanity can change this planet into a place that even if it isn't heaven on earth, it's getting closer. So what, you ask? Make your paradise however you will. In the end, though, it won't last. Everyone has the same fate. What's the phrase even the priests say, from dust you were made and to dust you will return? Game over, people.

Here's a thought for you. Maybe it sits in being too pragmatic for some, but there is, if not a totally different side, just another perspective on what life holds. At the center of what you say Jesus is and brings from God is Love. It's the highest value and ideal that could be achieved—good philosophy, no argument there. Its purpose is as said before, the betterment of the world, the greater good kind of thing. In the ideal world, all would commit to this greater good. Doing so would do much to eradicate this trouble of which you speak so much. Conflict, division, abusive grabs for control, all that would give way to a unity in which progress is based in love. When final breaths are taken, all can rest in having a legacy of life that continues on in others working out that love. Beyond that, that's it. Pass the baton. The race is over. Your turn is done.

As was said, this has been noted as a pragmatic perspective. Such a stoic approach seemingly would accomplish this greater good, the betterment of the world; that is the shared value. Yet this approach suffers from at least two insurmountable problems.

First, while humanity may hope for this ideal world, utopia is unattainable. Pragmaticism is based in realism, and realism takes a hard look at what is and what has been. Look around. Look at the world's history. For all the major movements and migrations in the world to build a brave new world, it never lasts. Call it what you will, there is an underlying force, an ever-mutating virus, that brings it down. Whenever this greater good appears, a destructive infection begins like a cancer to eat away and destroy its accomplishments. Don't bet your life on it. Even Jesus had a Judas.

Such an understanding, though, does not negate the effort to fight against this kind of trouble for the sake of others as well as one's own life. Without the battle, this brave-new-world ideal would have met a final fate long before this time. The struggle must go on, but to do so, it must be fueled with passion greater than just fear of pain and annihilation. The do-your-part-and-die philosophy has no passion other than that of survival of the species. Thus the second issue is embedded in the question, survival for what purpose?

Here is a perspective that reaches to what is beyond itself, beyond whatever humanity may achieve even in the name of a progressive love.

That's the point of Jesus's love. For him to die and end up as some kind of spiritual being floating beyond our planetary horizons would not accomplish what he came to do. Reversal is not just for people. Reversal is for all that life contains. That couple in the beginning needed to hear, "You won't die." This plan, this purpose, this power of Love is for this in all the ways it can be known—it must be known—by defeating the finality of death through resurrection powered by love. That Love embodied and operative in Jesus does the impossible, not only reversing the mind, body, and soul to that Love, but also to live life in that reversal, by full resurrection of both the body and the soul-spirit which hold life. For that end, Jesus physically rose from the dead as a living, breathing, restored, and renewed body. How did that happen? God knows. If anything, the process of Jesus's resurrection demonstrates how both the concept and full power of Love is beyond human understanding. But it had to happen because otherwise, if it couldn't happen for Jesus, all that's left is the trouble we've known and the trouble still to come.

With resurrection in Love, Jesus met that trouble. Born into trouble, bringing challenge by trouble, standing up to trouble, dying because of trouble, Jesus reversed the natural processes and understanding of life to defeat trouble in individuals and for all there is in the world.

And now our angry chorus, vented and subdued, also asks for the blessing.

Jesus, in all your goodness, you lived with us, knew our trouble, and promised so much in your life. We want it to be as you say, that as a child places a trusting hand in one who loves, we also want to follow you. Can this really be true, are you the Messiah, the one who will take away the worst of ourselves as well as what we love best about ourselves and make us new, born again you call it? Will you help us believe in you so we can believe in more than ourselves? Lord, help our unbelief.

Ever wonder if the efforts we make in life, we make harder than they have to be? Our ambitions, planning, and training take too much out of us and almost make us forget why we're doing this life in the first place. People who have grabbed the gold ring have sometimes felt that what they reached for was not enough, not worth the trouble. Something is missing, left out, not yet gained. Wealth, possessions, status, and power just don't fill that hole in the soul. Sad to think that even a life well lived has missed what life should be, is intended to be.

Yes, Jesus's life brought a call to live in love of God and neighbor. For something that could be so worthy of any life, his life was considered dangerous. Yet, he would not deter from his message. Despite whatever forces against him could be mustered, he never backed down. What was at stake was not his life. After all, he could have made some kind of miracle and escaped the fate of the cross. So why didn't he?

At the source of his message was this Love, but don't for an instant think it was just to get people to believe in his life, teachings, yes even resurrection after a brutal death on a cross. Before all that, at the beginning of the story, was the fullness of Love known as God. God could not be God without that which to Love. Therefore, God chose to have it overflow into a creation that culminated in a couple who sprang from this Love and was its total desire.

When that first couple turned away from this Love, interestingly God came looking for these creatures designed by this Love. "Where are you?" (Genesis 3:9). This Love would not abandon them despite how they had rejected it. From then, through the life of Jesus, even into today, Love still calls, "Where are you?"

Jesus's life was part of that calling, searching for these whom God loves. To affirm and accept his life, his call to reverse one's life to that of love for God and neighbor, is to enter into that Love. He lived to bring this Love, and he rose from a cold tomb to affirm that this Love will not die, will never end. God's love only asks for our love to answer this Love.

Two things are left for the chorus to decide. The first is the hardest kind of trouble. To get behind Jesus's "Follow me" is to resolve that you understand that "if you cling to your life, you will lose it." You will be in a place of eternal regret and no hope beyond your mortal self. "But if you give up your life for me," said Jesus, "you will find it" (Matthew 10:39). Your sense of soul and identity will be lost and then found in him. The ultimate reversal will be completed by Love.

Those who do, those who accept that exchanging one's life and trouble for a life that answers "Do you believe this?" affirmatively will receive another hard question. Recall that the night before Jesus died, he told his disciples, "If you love me, obey my commandments" (John 14:15). By this transformation centered in Love, take it to the world. Be all that Jesus asked by feeding sheep, reversing whatever troubles life brings and filling it with Love.

> I have told you all this so that you may have peace in me.
> Here on earth you will have many trials and sorrows.
> But take heart, because I have overcome the world.
> **—John 16:33**

Further Provocations for Your Consideration

1. The record of Jesus's life in many ways was written in the narrative form familiar to first-century readers, that of a Greek drama. He is portrayed as tragic hero, born into promise, endowed with superhuman powers, in conflict with the antithesis of his high moral character, flawed only by his refusal to be leveraged or compromise, and who died as a result of that conflict. Action in the narrative is enhanced by a chorus who observes and gives commentary both supportive and negative. When perceived in this art form, how does it speak to contemporary culture today?

_____

_____

_____

_____

2. Likewise, Jesus's life lends itself well in standing with both ancient and contemporary mythologies. The difference is, while couched in dramatic form, the records of his life also contend and assert a historical perspective not only of his life and death but also of his resurrection. How does this combination of drama and historical record as style contribute to the pervasiveness and persuasiveness of the narrative?

_____

_____

_____

3. "But to limit Jesus as merely a historical man or as almost a mythological figure is to kill him off better than the cross ever did." Why? How does this detract from not just his life record but also all that Jesus taught to his time and throughout time since he lived?

_____

_____

_____

4. The pragmatists and stoics take on the trouble of the world but dispassionately face the end of life with a finality denying the eternal. Jesus says that there's more in a God-love beyond what humanity can achieve on its own, reversing its trouble which impacts life as known now, that is, life after death. What do these perspectives have in common, and where do they differ? Which requires the greater courage, faith, or belief?

_____

_____

_____

5. "Jesus physically rose from the dead as a living, breathing, restored, and renewed body. How did that happen? God knows. If anything, the process of Jesus's resurrection demonstrates how both the concept and full power of Love is beyond human understanding." Culture today seeks and sings of love constantly. How does this premise that Jesus's Love, the Love of God, is such a powerful source that it can reverse the finality of death compare with the kind of love people are told or think is necessary for happiness and life-fulfillment?

_____

_____

_____

_____

6. The Love of God is often expressed as unconditional Love. What does that mean? Does it grant measures of tolerance, or do boundaries contradict the unconditionality of that kind of love? Do boundaries impede love or protect it? Explain.

_____

_____

_____

_____

7. The subtitle of this book is *Considerations Before You Walk Away.* What new considerations have you encountered about Jesus from this reading?

_____

_____

_____

8. This presentation of Jesus in a loose context of dramatic structure deliberately progressed without the inclusion of specific church denominational theology and without addressing the criticisms of contemporary church positions. Even so, to what extent have these influenced or impacted your willingness to accept Jesus's claims on your life and follow him?

_____

_____

_____

_____

9. It must be asked again: "I am the resurrection and the life. Anyone who believes in me will live, even after dying. Everyone who lives in me and believes in me will never ever die. Do you believe this?" (John 11:25–26). What's your answer?

_____

_____

_____

_____

_____

_____

After Words:

Provocations from Others

Want more? Disclaimer here. This book is not a tell-all. Not even close. Jesus's good friend and disciple wrote in his report, "Jesus also did many other things. If they were all written down, I suppose the whole world could not contain the books that would be written" (John 21:25). However, based on what the writers of Matthew, Mark, Luke, and John did say about Jesus, plenty of other books have been written.

It must be said, no one stands alone in the formation of faith. True, reading as close as possible to the original sources about Jesus from those who knew him and his followers is primary. Yet, it must be recognized that much of faith is built on the struggles of those who have been on this journey and wrestled with questions and doubts so others don't have as hard a time. The trouble with Jesus is that his life compels his followers to tell their stories of that journey and pass on what nuggets of wisdom and strength they have gleaned by doing so. I thank God for them, and I pray that this book may be that for all who take the trouble to read it.

So, in honor and fairness to all those who have struggled with Jesus's story and claims, below is a small list of resources I recommend for those who would allow Jesus-trouble into their considerations of where he has a place in one's soul and life purpose. Some of these resources are specific to the life and times and teachings of Jesus, while others are broader in discussion of God and the Bible. Some of these are classics, even bestsellers in the Christian canon and require deep contemplation in dedicated reading. Others are lesser known, easy reads but no less challenging to Jesus's narrative. All have found a place on my bookshelf from time to time, and some have traveled, finding homes in hands beyond my own. Suffice it to say, all of these have merit in regard to who Jesus was and how he is accepted today.

First, though, I recommend that you find a Bible you like in a format you will use. The Bible is available everywhere from apps for phones and tablets to paperback and leather-bound volumes in large print. Whichever you choose, let it be one that you can highlight, mark with notes, or leave questions on the page. (God will appreciate the exchange.) Audible versions are also available. (Good for those who need to yell back.)

Select a Bible in a translation that you will read. While lovers of sixteenth century Shakespearian literature may revel in the Kings James Version, modern translations of the Hebrew and Greek deliver the message also. The New Revised Standard Version (NRSV), New International Version (NIV), and Contemporary English Bible (CEB) are reliable selections. The Message, a total paraphrase of the Bible by Eugene Peterson, is popular for its creative poetic style. In this book, I mainly used the New Living Translation (NLT) because of its readability. Some modern translations also strive to be gender inclusive. So while God is referred to as "He" when directly translated from the original texts, Jesus came to save both women and men. (Thank God!)

Bibles are also available with additional study notes and commentary. If you are willing to move forward in your considerations, this is important. Study notes will provide additional contextual information, sometimes maps of the geography, and some cross-references. (No, Jesus was not the first to say love God and neighbor.) Such notes will help you find these kinds of things.

Commentaries can be specific to the reader: Women's Bibles, Kid's Bibles, Teen's Bibles, and more. I use the Life Recovery Bible written for those who have addictive habits they are trying to overcome. (Like who hasn't something in their life they don't need to shake off?)

With the Good Book in your hands, read it. I recommend reading it every day. Start with the section called the New Testament. In its first four "books" is Jesus's story. Everything else before it in the Bible (called the Old Testament) is the prequel to Jesus, and everything else following is the sequel. So start with the most important part, the four Gospels, which focus on Jesus and the gospel (good news) he came to present. From there you can decide where to go next.

You'll find in your online search for a Bible plenty of study books that have various themes. Those are great, but more important is to connect with other people who will sit with you and this Jesus-trouble. Here are two places you can go online for personal help:

- **Alpha:** Search www.alphausa.org. If you like English accents, this one is for you. Actually, you don't have to have a preference to join. "Alpha is a series of sessions exploring the Christian faith, typically run over eleven weeks. Each talk looks at a different question around faith and is designed to create conversation." That was right from the website. You can search for a group in your area, or if it's better for your life or lifestyle, there are online sessions available. What's great about this group is you don't have to say a thing or you can say anything. At the least, the questions they raise are good for consideration, and they also feed you fairly well if you attend an in-person group.
- **Celebrate Recovery:** Search www.celebraterecovery.com. You are likely familiar with Alcoholics Anonymous and twelve-step groups. What distinguishes CR is that it names Jesus as its higher power. Yes, you'll find in these groups people who struggle with addic-

tions. But more so, this program is for persons with all kinds of "hurts, habits, and hang-ups." If your consideration of Jesus-trouble is coupled with those kinds of issues that trip up your life, this is one of the best places you can go to engage those issues.

Numerous Christian books can provide summaries, insights, answers, and inspiration concerning Jesus, his life, and teachings. Here are some that I've found especially beneficial:

Thurman, Howard. 1976. *Jesus and the Disinherited*. Boston, MA: Beacon Press. This book gives a perspective of the losers Jesus chose and loved. Just read the "Foreword" by Vincent Harding. You won't put the book down from there.

Paul, Greg. 2004. *God in the Alley: Being and Seeing Jesus in a Broken World*. Colorado Springs, CO: Waterbrook Press. If you think you can be like Jesus by helping the losers and the poor but walk away like nothing happened and not be changed, then don't follow this guy's example. But read it anyway just to see how it's done.

McGrath, James F. 2021. *What Jesus Learned from Women*. Eugene, OR: Cascade Books. This book gives a creative narration that's fully researched in the historical context of the biblical passages relating to the women Jesus knew, healed, and for whom he was a powerful advocate.

Alcorn, Randy. 1989. *Money, Possessions and Eternity*. Wheaton, IL: Tyndale House. This resource is comprehensive and convicting for those who take seriously what Jesus said about money. This one will also cost you, and not just for the price of the book.

Cloud, Henry, and John Townsend. 1992. *Boundaries*. Grand Rapids, MI: Zondervan. Jesus stressed relationship with God and neighbor. And this can't happen without healthy boundaries cemented in love. This must-read has been a bestseller for good reason.

Kalas, J. Ellsworth. 1992. *Parables from the Back Side: Bible Stories with a Twist*. Nashville, TN: Abingdon Press. Jesus was a master storyteller. This book delightfully demonstrates how Jesus packed these tales with relatable lessons not always examined on the first read. From here, check out Kalas's other books in this series From the Back Side.

MacNutt, Francis. 1974, 2002. *Healing*. Notre Dame, IN: Ava Maria Press. Do you think miracles stopped after the first century? Read the accounts of healings from this former Roman Catholic priest who lived his life dedicated to his belief in the person of Jesus and what that faith can accomplish.

O'Reilly, Bill, and Martin Dugard. 2013. *Killing Jesus*. New York: Henry Holt and Co. The authors provide thorough research on the historical and political context that came into play leading to Jesus's crucifixion. Raw accounts make it real.

Willimon, William H. 2006. *Thank God It's Friday: Encountering the Last Seven Words from the Cross*. Nashville, TN: Abingdon Press. Not a difficult read, but not an easy read either. Take each chapter slowly. Maybe even read each chapter more than once before progressing to the next one. Listen to these last words Jesus spoke from his cross.

Lewis, C. S. 1997. *Mere Christianity*. New York: Scribner. Such a classic this is, you'll find it on your preferred online book-shopping website in multiple editions by several publishers. All attest to how this book, first published in 1952, is not going away. It also takes a dedicated reading, worth it for the one who wants an understanding of what Christianity is supposed to be. (Not saying this is how all those who claim it really live it. So what? The Christian life is a marathon, not a sprint, as they say.)

Huffman, Eric. 2021. *Scripture and the Skeptic: Miracles, Myths, and Doubts of Biblical Proportions*. Nashville, TN: Abingdon Press. Good presentation with a sense of humor and relatable illustrations. You can tell from the title that it discusses the entire Bible, not only the Jesus narratives. It's worth a look without needing to devote tons of time. (At least the first time through.)

Metaxas, Eric. 2005. *Everything You Always Wanted to Know about God (But Were Afraid to Ask)*. Colorado Springs, CO: WaterBrook Press. Gives a great presentation in the Q&A format that each chapter utilizes. Very readable as well. Again, this book is broad in scope, but the chapter titles quickly give sight to the question most pressing. Also, Metaxas has a follow-up book (2007) with more questions covered. *Everything Else You Always Wanted to Know about God (But Were Afraid to Ask)*.

Strobel, Lee. 2016. *The Case for Christ: A Journalist's Personal Investigation of the Evidence for Jesus*. Grand Rapids, MI: Zondervan. Considered a gold standard for apologetics. Yes, there is a movie by the same title. Still, read the book for more in-depth arguments for Jesus's life and resurrection.

Finally, if you'd like more of *The Trouble with Jesus* in blog form, you'll find me at https://constancehastings.com, with each blog usually around a five-minute read. Comments, questions, this doesn't make sense . . . whatever your response to Jesus in your considerations is welcomed.

Acknowledgments

The Lord will fulfill his purpose for me;
your love, O Lord, endures forever.
—Psalm 138:8

Left to my own ambitions, my life would not have taken the path it has. Yet the making of *The Trouble with Jesus: Considerations Before You Walk Away* is in many ways the culmination of the one I was given. God's hand of grace and formation not only gave me life work and relationships which I cherish but also brought about this book through those experiences.

The Trouble with Jesus: Considerations Before You Walk Away is not of my own invention. I had no intention to write a book. Sure, there was a time when I worked as a freelance reporter, and I had many articles published in newsletters. None of that, however, entailed the investment of time, the sacrifice of who I thought I was meant to be, and the wrestling I needed to make in the consideration of the life of Jesus Christ.

What you hold in your hands came about in the not surprising request of a church women's group. Aldersgate United Methodist Women approached me about leading a Saturday morning Bible study. With a lifetime of biblical studies, seminary training, ordination, and leadership in churches and throughout the Peninsula-Delaware Conference, I should have been able to just pull out a scripture and message. Didn't happen.

For two months or so, I struggled with what would have spiritual impact on these dedicated, smart, well read, professional, church ladies. No passage in all of the sixty-six books of the Bible inspired me to go with it. Finally, one day I just looked up and said out loud, "The trouble is with Jesus." No celestial chimes rang out, but I knew that would be it.

The Trouble with Jesus began with a three-hour class. Soon I realized I had the outline of a book. The skeptical voice in the book was familiar in my head as well. As Jesus lived in the midst of trouble, there would be, and still is, challenge to him and his message. I could see the pages forming around it.

Except—when you work hard and stretch yourself in many places, something has to give. But the call to write would not go away. I learned many years before how this insistent nudge meant God had another plan for what I was meant to do. Six years later, I turned over many positions and projects in which I served and followed my husband to Florida. We told people that our move was to be near our son and his wife, which truly was a joy. But I agreed to go only if I could have time and space to write. My family generously gave it to me.

Like many novices, I thought I only had to crank out the pages, send them off to an agent/publisher, and God would take it from there. Lord have mercy, but there is more to writing a book than this former teacher of great literature realized. God pushed me down that path with great mentors and coaches to learn how to structure my writing, promote what was coming through blog writing and garnering subscribers, and what form of publishing would best afford the book in print, digital, and audio forms.

Specifically, from my knees I thank God for Rhonda Robinson and her Scribe Tribe who developed my website and brought about the blog; Amanda Rooker of Split Seed for her manuscript editing as a confirmed skeptic; Bill Watkins of Literary Solutions for applying his immense biblical insight and strong theological perspectives, not to mention skill in formatting and structuring the book for publication; W. Terry Whalin of Morgan James Publishing for leading me into the publishing process; and all of the team members of Morgan James Publishing for their expertise in taking *The Trouble with Jesus: Considerations Before You Walk Away* from a holy nudge to book in hand.

Beyond these, I also ask blessing upon all who have prayed for this book in its creation: family, life groups, Bible study friends, and pastors who have passed on inspiration in their own writings and sermons. Standing next to them are my former students and counseling clients whose lives have enriched mine with their stories of struggle in their own kinds of trouble. Subscribers to my blog have given me support and encouragement along the way. I believe God put all of you in my life for the specific reason of teaching me how wide, long, high, and deep his love really is (Ephesians 3:18).

Beside me in this journey, my husband Robert (Bob) Hastings has been a little patient, tolerant of the trouble I've been, and an example of love in marriage that brought me into a community of the faithful (sometimes known as church), affirmed the gifts given to me, and gave me to God so that together we can be not just good people but greater together in who we are. Honey, I love you and thank God for giving you to me.

Again, not the path I would have chosen but the one I was given. Life has had directions that were none of my own doing except that I live in the grace that nudges, calls, pushes me for that purpose. Like everyone else, I've wrestled against it. Yet, the trouble with Jesus is he doesn't give up even when we want to walk away. Thank God for that.

The Lord will fulfill his purpose for me. Likewise, God will do for you. Thus, by God's will and glory, in the movement, activity, and power of the Holy Spirit, and because of the forgiveness, mercy, goodness, love, and grace known in the holy and blessed name of Jesus, I humbly give *The

Trouble with Jesus: Considerations Before You Walk Away to you, faithful doubter. May the ways God leads you to understand and believe in Jesus, the Son of God, and the trouble he brings surprise you, shape you, deepen you, and transform you forever and ever.

The peace of Christ be with you. Shalom.
—Connie Hastings

About the Author

Constance Hastings is the granddaughter of Italian immigrants and Georgia sharecroppers.

Most of her life she has lived in Delaware, the Mid-Atlantic region, until a few years ago when she and her husband decided to split residences between Wilmington, Delaware and Jacksonville, Florida so as to be near both their children.

She attended a small Christian school through the eighth grade for not quite the right reasons. Her family lived in the inner city during school desegregation, and so to keep her out of that conflict, her parents sent her to Wilmington Christian School close to home. She wasn't the typical student there. Her father owned a bar, and her mother took her to Sunday school and, when old enough, just dropped her off to attend on her own.

To the school's credit, they loved her and taught her well. While learning enough of the usual academics, she excelled at Bible study, putting those kids whose dads were preachers and missionaries to shame. There she took on for herself a belief in Jesus as the Son of God.

She studied literature as an undergraduate, and then followed up by earning a Master of Instruction at the University of Delaware. Connie feels that she learned to write when teaching high school composition. Though a lover of great authors, she became a teacher of the disadvantaged as a high school and community college instructor, for which she was honored with an Excellence in Teaching award.

As a freelance journalist, she covered small town events as well as a presidential speech at the White House and received numerous awards.

Life took on a surprising direction when she had a spiritual calling to enter ministry with a focus on mental health counseling as an ordained deacon in The Methodist Church. That second master's degree in community counseling at Wilmington University and seminary training were enthralling, stretching her mind in places she would never have known without its challenges. In some ways, though, she also found that this part of her education was an extension of what she had known before.

Her clients invited her into the stories of their lives, not unlike the great literature she loves, and she was privileged to walk with them as they negotiated their paths. She considers people who work through the counseling process no less than courageous heroes.

Ordination in a mainline denomination really didn't fit with this background. She had never been a member of a church, likely didn't take communion until she was in her twenties, and wasn't baptized until her son was born. But God knows why, this is how her life happened.

She comes to doctrine, dogma, and the biblical text with an outsider's sense of what insiders know, grateful for that edge to which she writes and engages.

A free ebook edition is available with the purchase of this book.

To claim your free ebook edition:

1. Visit MorganJamesBOGO.com
2. Sign your name CLEARLY in the space
3. Complete the form and submit a photo of the entire copyright page
4. You or your friend can download the ebook to your preferred device

Morgan James
BOGO™

A **FREE** ebook edition is available for you or a friend with the purchase of this print book.

CLEARLY SIGN YOUR NAME ABOVE

Instructions to claim your free ebook edition:
1. Visit MorganJamesBOGO.com
2. Sign your name CLEARLY in the space above
3. Complete the form and submit a photo of this entire page
4. You or your friend can download the ebook to your preferred device

Print & Digital Together Forever.

Snap a photo

Free ebook

Read anywhere

Printed in the USA
CPSIA information can be obtained
at www.ICGtesting.com
JSHW082043140624
64842JS00003B/31

9 781636 983387